CREATIVE THINKING AND PROBLEM SOLVING IN GIFTED EDUCATION

JOHN F. FELDHUSEN
Purdue University

DONALD J. TREFFINGER
State University College at Buffalo

KENDALL/HUNT PUBLISHING COMPANY
2460 Kerper Boulevard, Dubuque, Iowa 52001

Originally entitled: TEACHING CREATIVE THINKING
AND PROBLEM SOLVING

"This work was developed in part under a grant from the National Institute of
Education, Department of Health, Education, and Welfare. However, the content does
not necessarily reflect the position or policy of that Agency, and no official endorsement
of these materials shall be inferred."

Printed in the United States of America

B   402155   01

CONTENTS

LIST OF REVIEWS IN CHAPTER SIX

Instructional Material

PREFACE

We were thrilled by the excellent reception to the first edition of this book. Hundreds of teachers in cities throughout the United States told us that they found the book to be a valuable guide in developing plans to teach creative thinking and problem solving. However, it is obvious to us that the book has been especially valuable to teachers in gifted education programs. Both of us have attended numerous workshops, conferences and conventions on gifted education, and it was chiefly in that context that we learned about the great need of teachers for such guidance in developing gifted education programs.

We were also pleased to learn that our reviews of instructional material were a valuable guide to school personnel seeking material for gifted education programs. We learned that many schools simply ordered all the materials we recommended.

Thus, the second edition of our book focuses more directly on the gifted. There is an entire chapter on teaching creative thinking and problem solving to the gifted, creative and talented. Other chapters have been substantially revised, especially Chapter Four, "Methods of Teaching Creativity and Problem Solving." Our reviews of instructional material, as presented in Chapter Six, have also been greatly revised. Many new materials have been added. Some have been dropped.

The search for new instructional material was aided greatly by the service of graduate student Becki Utigard. She did an excellent job searching the literature and helping us evaluate materials.

We hope that this new edition of our book will help teachers do a better job of teaching creativity and problem solving to the gifted, creative and talented. These youth are our great hope for the future. Sound programs of gifted education will meet their special needs and help them bring their potential to fruition in the arts, professions, business, government, and sciences.

John F. Feldhusen
Donald J. Treffinger

Chapter 1

TEACHING STUDENTS TO THINK

The first purpose of this book is to help teachers teach students how to think and especially how to think creatively and solve problems. Much time in the classroom is spent teaching information and basic skills in reading and mathematics. Very little is used to teach students how to use information and basic skills in thinking, solving problems, or creating new ideas.

A second purpose of this book is to help teachers learn how to teach creative thinking and problem solving to gifted, creative and talented children. Gifted children have high intellectual and academic ability. Creative children have the ability to create new ideas. Talented children have special abilities in one area such as music, art or drama. All these gifted children need special help in developing their gifted potential.

Creative thinking is the ability to think of a lot of ideas where there is a problem or a need for ideas (Gallagher, 1975). It is also being able to think of many different ideas, to think of unique or original ideas, and to develop or elaborate ideas. Sometimes it is asking good questions which clarify a problem. It is also being able to translate ideas into forms of communication or expression which make it possible for other people to grasp the ideas or solution to problems. Thus, it is necessary to find words or use art media, music, drama, or movement to express our ideas, solutions, or feelings.

Problem solving is a complex set of skills and abilities. Guilford and his associates (Guilford and Hoepfner, 1971; Merrifield, Guilford, Christensen, and Frick, 1962) have carried out extensive research on problem-solving abilities. They conclude that there is no single problem-solving-ability. Instead, there are a number of abilities involved in the complete problem-solving process. They concluded from their factor analytic studies of problem solving that the following abilities are major cognitive functions in problem solving: (1) thinking rapidly of several characteristics of a given object or situation; (2) classifying objects or ideas; (3) perceiving relationships; (4) thinking of alternative outcomes; (5) listing characteristics of a goal; and (6) producing logical solutions (1971, pages 104–107)

We have combined creativity and problem solving into a single complex concept following the model proposed by Guilford and his associates. Many discrete creative abilities such as fluency, flexibility, and originality, while measureable and trainable separately, are in reality indispensable components of realistic and complex problem solving behavior. Puzzle type problems might involve only restricted logical thinking abilities. Real life problem solving is really creative problem solving in that it requires a wide range of creative, conceptual and logical thinking abilities.

It is a frequently expressed goal of American education, at all levels, to foster cognitive growth among children, and particularly to help children think creatively and to become better problem solvers. In their text, *Teaching for Thinking,* Raths, Wasserman, Jonas, and Rothstein (1967) stated the case, in general terms, as follows:

> There is a widespread verbal recognition of the importance of thinking. We want our children to be able to think for themselves, to be self-directing, considerate, and thoughtful. In situations which are new to them we hope they will be able to apply knowledge which they have gained in the past. (p. 1)

The importance of research on creativity and problem solving more specifically has been described by Parnes (1967), Torrance (1965, 1967), Torrance and Myers (1970), Guilford (1967) and others. Guilford has described the importance of creative problem solving in education in an especially provocative way:

> It is apparent that the solutions to numerous human problems are dependent upon education of the world's population. . . . An informed people . . . is a creative, problem-solving people (1967, p. 12).

In an increasingly complex, ever changing, challenging and problem-ridden world, people of all ages have great need to be good creative thinkers and good problem solvers. However, the greatest hope for improving thinking lies with children in school. It is easier to arrange the conditions in school to help children learn how to think than to try to change adults, most of whom are no longer involved in formal education.

Children from some economically disadvantaged and low-income minority families are more likely than middle class children to face serious problems in many aspects of their lives. Thus they have a special need to become good thinkers, good problem solvers. Accordingly a special effort was made to find methods and materials which would be especially useful for teachers of children from economically disadvantaged and low-income minority families. However, it is likely that all teachers will find the information useful in improving their teaching of thinking, creative thinking, problem solving, critical thinking, and inquiry.

An attempt was made to assemble and evaluate a large amount of information about teaching materials and methods, especially for teaching creative

2

thinking and problem solving. However, it was found that such materials are often closely related to the teaching topics of inquiry and critical thinking. Therefore, these topics are dealt with in reviews whenever some aspect of creativity or problem solving was identified as a part of critical thinking and inquiry.

It was also recognized very early in the project that most of the time in typical classrooms is devoted to the usual curricular or subject matter areas such as social studies, language arts and reading, science and mathematics. Thus, it was decided that it might be best to give teachers information on how to teach thinking within regular subjects as much as possible.

Finally, it was recognized that a lot of guidance and direction from teachers on the job would be needed. Thus, nearly one hundred teachers in Atlanta, Kansas City, Indianapolis, and Los Angeles were interviewed. In addition, questionnaires were given to hundreds of other teachers in grades kindergarten to six. Thus, a great deal was learned about teachers' needs, problems and concerns in trying to teach children to think.

An Overview of This Book

Chapter 2 discusses the special problems of teaching creative thinking and problem solving to students from economically disadvantaged families and minority homes. Several conceptions of the disadvantaged student and of intellectual deficit are presented.

Chapter 3 is concerned with teaching creativity and problem solving to gifted, creative and talented students. They have special need for high level development of their abilities in creativity and problem solving.

Chapter 4 presents information about teaching methods or techniques which can be readily adapted by the teacher to fit any grade level and subject area. Nothing need be purchased. These are methods and techniques for teaching creative thinking, problem solving, and inquiry. Often no special materials are needed. No AV equipment is needed. However, it will usually be necessary to adapt the technique to fit a particular grade level or subject matter.

Chapter 5 provides more specific directions on how to get a project started in the classroom. It gives detailed directions for creativity and problem-solving exercises and procedures for implementing them in the classroom. Chapter 5 also presents guidelines for developing learning modules or packages for teaching creative thinking and problem solving.

Chapter 6 presents the descriptions of published *teaching material* for specific grade levels and subject areas. It is divided into two main sections. The first section includes reviews of commercially published materials dealing with creativity and problem solving. The second section includes reviews of books that can be used, either through the suggestions that they give on methods of teaching creative thinking or problem solving' or by actually using them as stimulus materials. The best way to use this chapter is as a reference source to familiarize yourself with the great variety of materials that are available. In this way you will be better able to choose materials to fit your specific needs.

Special Classes for the Gifted, Creative, and Talented

Many cities throughout the United States are organizing special programs for gifted, creative, and talented students. In some of these programs the regular classroom teacher is assisted by a resource teacher in developing activities in the classroom. In others, the students meet after school or Saturdays with a special resource teacher. Still others set up special classes for the gifted, creative, and talented. Whatever the administrative arrangement, the teachers must search for and develop materials and methods which will stimulate intellectual and creative growth in these students. The ideas presented in this book are intended to help these teachers in their work with gifted, creative, and talented students.

Summary

The first purpose of this book is to help teachers learn about promising materials, methods and techniques for teaching creative thinking and problem solving in their classrooms. The second purpose is to help teachers learn how to teach creative thinking and problem solving to gifted, creative and talented students. In many schools teachers are developing broad new methods for open and individualized instruction. Most of the material reviewed and presented in this book for teaching creative thinking and problem solving will work well in open and individualized classrooms. Creative thinking and problem solving are intensely personal and individual experiences which thrive in an open classroom climate. However, teachers who maintain a more traditional classroom organization will also find that many of the materials and methods are adaptable to their needs and organization. A wealth of good ideas and good materials is available for teachers who are industrious, intelligent, creative, and motivated to apply them in their classrooms.

REFERENCES
Gallagher, J.J. *Teaching the Gifted Child (2nd Ed.)* Boston: Allyn and Bacon, 1975, Ch. 9.
Guilford, J.P. *The Nature of Human Intelligence.* New York: McGraw-Hill, 1967.
Guilford, J.P. and Hoepfner, R. *The Analysis of Intelligence.* New York: McGraw-Hill, 1971.

Merrifield, P.R., Guilford, J.P., Christensen, P.R., and Frick, J.W. *The Role of Intellectual Factors in Problem Solving.* Psychological Monographs, 1962, 76, No. 10.

Parnes, S.J. *Creative Behavior Guidebook.* New York: Scribner's, 1967.

Raths, L.E., Wasserman, S., Jonas, A., and Rothstein, A.M. *Teaching for Thinking: Theory and Application.* Columbus: Charles E. Merrill, 1967.

Torrance, E.P. *Rewarding Creative Behavior.* Englewood Cliffs, N.J.: Prentice-Hall, 1965.

Torrance, E.P. Epilogue: Creativity in American Education, 1865–1965. In Gowan, J.C., Demos, G.D., and Torrance, E.P. (eds) *Creativity; Its Educational Implications.* New York: John Wiley, 1967.

Torrance, E.P., and Myers, R.E. *Creative Learning and Teaching.* New York: Dodd, Mead and Co., 1970.

Chapter 2

TEACHING CREATIVE THINKING AND PROBLEM SOLVING TO THE GIFTED, CREATIVE AND TALENTED

Gifted, creative and talented students have several kinds of immediate and long range needs. Perhaps their major long range needs are to be able to realize their full career potential and to be able to experience a sense of personal fulfillment or self actualization in maturity. For students with the highest levels of potential, we expect careers that will result in high level creative productions, inventions, or solutions to major societal problems. The *immediate* needs of the gifted may be to have educational and personal experiences which will eventually facilitate their progress toward the long range goals, help them develop important skills, and yet provide immediate happiness and satisfaction.

What kinds of instructional activities serve those immediate needs of the gifted, creative and talented? We can readily identify nine different kinds of activities which can serve the needs of gifted, creative, and talented students in school. Some of these can also be served by parents and other agencies outside of the school, of course. These activites are:

1. maximum achievement of basic skills and conceptual understanding in school subjects
2. learning activities appropriate to the student's level of academic achievements
3. a large fund of information about diverse topics
4. exposure to a variety of potential fields of study and occupations
5. development of awareness and acceptance of their own capacities, interests, and needs
6. experience in creative thinking and problem solving
7. stimulation to pursue higher level goals and aspirations
8. development of independence and self-direction in learning
9. experience in relating effectively with other people

The first need is for maximum achievement of basic skills and conceptual understanding in school subjects. This need is closely linked to the second, learning activities appropriate to the student's level of academic achievement.

7

The pace and depth of instruction in most classrooms is geared to a hypothetical "average" student. Often there may be no opportunity for the gifted child to pursue skills and concepts at the deeper level for which he/she has the ability. For the gifted student who has managed to learn at an accelerated pace, this means engaging in classroom activities well below his/her appropriate achievement levels. Gifted students suffer particularly in this respect in mathematics and science. Often the door is open in language arts and social studies for the student to forge ahead even without help from the teacher. Sometimes the help comes from parents or outside agencies, sometimes simply from books and reading.

Individualized basic instruction, appropriate enrichment programs, and formal acceleration procedures can and should be developed for gifted students who are advanced achievers. Figure 2.1 suggests some approaches at the different grade levels. Teachers and school administrators are often reluctant to accept any forms of acceleration, but they are needed for gifted students who are highly advanced achievers.

The gifted also have great need to master basic skills in mathematics, science and language arts to facilitate their overall learning in school. Language arts skills are especially vital in all learning activities which involve reading and writing. Gifted students can do much to facilitate their own learning if they can master the basic skills and use them in further learning situations.

The third need of gifted students is for a large fund of information. Many gifted students are ardent seekers of information. They read encyclopedias, dictionaries, atlases, and fact books as well as general literature and become great storehouses of seemingly idle information. In truth such an information reservoir can be the base for much creative thinking. Creatively gifted students can call forth varied information to develop many possibilities, to form new associations, and to think of unusual ideas in solving problems. A large storehouse of information seems to be indispensable.

This need for a large fund of information can be met through a variety of experiences in interaction with people, through reading, and through opportunities to explore, try out, and experience directly. Teachers and parents need to provide abundant opportunities for gifted children for reading, for travel, for visits to historical and cultural sites, art experiences, and interactions with people. There should also be much emphasis on information transmission in any special classes or individualized work for the gifted.

The fourth need is for exposure to a variety of potential fields of study and occupations. These experiences should come quite early for gifted students. In part they constitute career education, and many schools are instituting such programs. However, gifted students' needs go well beyond conventional career education programs. They need much exposure to higher

| For Whom? | (a) | Children who are at or above the 95% ile on standardized achievement tests for initial screening. |
| | (b) | Children who are two or more grade levels above grade placement on standardized achievement tests. |

Primary Level Provision?	(a)	Individualized or small group activity to provide advanced instruction in math, science, language arts or social studies.
	(b)	Early admission to school.
	(c)	Grade advancement.

| Upper Elementary? | (a) | Special accelerated groups for instruction in math, science, English and social studies. |
| | (b) | Early admission to higher level high school courses. |

High School?	(a)	Special accelerated groups for instruction in math, science, English and social studies.
	(b)	Early admission to advanced high school courses.
	(c)	Organize college level courses to be offered in high school.
	(d)	Release students to take college courses in vicinity.
	(e)	Special summer programs of courses at college and universities.

Figure 2.1. Acceleration for very high achievers

level occupations, art careers and biographies of creatively productive people to help them become aware of their own potential and possible goals to strive for.

Activities in this area are complementary to those in the fifth area, development of awareness and acceptance of their capacities, interests, and needs. Many gifted students fail to realize and understand their own abilities, aptitudes and achievements. This self knowledge is critically related to the exploration of careers and fields of study. Gifted students must come to see optimum links between their own abilities and potential careers.

The next area of instructional activities, the sixth, is creative thinking and problem solving. Gifted students need activities in this area to help them expand their capacity for high level invention, inquiry and discovery. Full use of abilities in achieving maximum potentials means that many gifted students will produce new, unique, original contributions in their fields as adults. Early experience in creative thinking and problem solving paves the way, helps the children learn how to use divergent thinking capacities and creative problem solving. They should also become aware of the potency of creative thinking and problem solving as "mental tools" to achieve new heights of invention and production.

In the seventh area, gifted students need stimulation to pursue higher level goals and aspirations commensurate with their potential. Teachers and parents can encourage them and successful adults can serve as models. Gifted students growing up in poverty or minority family situations may lack both encouragement and models. The school may have to become the principal source of those influences. Persistent and helpful mentors can help meet this need. Teachers can give much encouragement. In a sense this seventh need is for motivational stimulation commensurate with the gifted student's potential. Highly productive adults have often identified their goals very early in life and have been able to concentrate their efforts during the school years toward achievement of those goals. The motivational intensity and level must be extremely high for the gifted if they are to achieve their full potential.

The eighth goal addresses the need for gifted students to learn how to manage and direct their own learning, and to become effective in independent inquiry. In part, this involves learning how to use methodological and research skills and library or reference materials. But it also means learning, at home and in school, how to "take command" of their own learning. Parents and teachers should not expect gifted students to know how to do these things naturally or spontaneously. They must learn how to set goals, identify and locate resources, formulate and carry out plans, and evaluate their work. Adults should also expect gifted students to develop these skills *gradually* (Treffinger & Barton, 1980).

Finally, the ninth goal deals with relating effectively with other people. We do not want to encourage the development of adults who are intellectual "giants" although socially or interpersonally inept. It is important for individuals to be able to function skillfully and happily with many other persons of varying ages, interests, and abilities.

The Role of Creativity in Enrichment Programs

In delineating the special needs of gifted, creative and talented students, we have explicitly suggested that experiences in creative thinking and problem solving are essential for gifted, creative and talented students because we want to pave the way for high level success in these skills in maturity. We assume that the necessary mix in maturity includes:

1. strong basic abilities
2. skill in creative thinking and problem solving
3. facilitative environmental conditions to foster high level creative production

We further assume that the experience in creative thinking and problem solving should begin early and be promoted both in school and in the home. The Goertzels (1978) have documented well the role of home and family relationships in the lives of eminent contributors to society.

This need to teach the skills of creative thinking and problem solving and to provide experience therein cuts across the entire range of a child's development from infancy (Starkweather, 1971) to adulthood (Parnes, Noller & Biondi, 1977). Thus, it obviously is not the kind of learning which can be neatly encapsulated in a semester or year of study. Rather, through a continuous program beginning in childhood we hope that basic skills and life styles which facilitate creative thinking and problem solving can be acquired, sustained, and strengthened.

The three-stage model for creative enrichment programs (Feldhusen & Kolloff, 1978), Renzulli's Triad model (1977), and a creative learning model (Treffinger, 1979b) all provide guidelines for several levels of creative thinking and problem solving activities for the gifted. Basic skills and strategies of creative thinking are presented as underlying or fundamentals to be learned as a prelude to the highest level of activity, independent project and problem solving activity. These models stress that there are some relatively discrete skills to be learned such as ideational fluency and elaboration in writing and design. Gifted children must especially have this underpinning to assure their later success in higher level creative activities. These basic level abilities also include mastery of drawing and writing, reading, and quantitative skills. Some of these can be acquired through the regular classroom activity and individ-

11

ualization of learning there. But others, especially those related to creative thinking, problem solving, and independent activity, are dealt with more effectively in special programming for the gifted.

The second level in these models calls for the provision of experience in broader strategies of creative thinking, problem solving, and project activity. One specific example involves application of the Creative Problem Solving model (Noller, 1977; Noller, Treffinger & Houseman, 1979; Parnes, Noller & Biondi, 1977). Synectics, morphological analysis, and research and inquiry strategies are all taught and experienced in this second stage. Creative enrichment models for the gifted all stress some form of these experiences as being fundamental parts of special programs.

The third stage of creative activity for the gifted calls for the highest level possible of creative, productive activity. Gifted, creative and talented students can work independently or in small groups at this level using basic skills and strategies acquired in stages one and two in addressing realistic complex problems. This is perhaps the ultimate strategy level. Teachers, parents, and/or mentors act as resource persons, guides, and stimulators, while the student(s) take(s) the initiative. One child may be writing about dinosaurs, while other children are writing a play which they will produce, writing a series of haiku poems, or studying rat reinforcement behaviors. Several students are also designing their own micro-computer. These are all appropriate stage three activities for gifted, creative and talented students.

It can, of course, be argued that these are appropriate activities for *all* children and should be taught to all children in regular classes. This argument is partly true but it neglects gifted students' needs for appropriately higher level, more abstract, and more challenging experiences in these activities. The levels of experience for the gifted might prove frustrating for average or *less* able youngsters. However, some teachers who conduct creative enrichment activities with the gifted in their classes report that less able youngsters can sometimes work effectively with gifted students in such project activity and that both, the gifted and the less able, profit from the experience.

In addition to the fundamental learnings at the three stages or levels, creative enrichment can also serve as a vehicle for attainment of other learning needs of the gifted as set forth earlier in this chapter, particularly the needs for:

1. maximum achievement of basic skills and conceptual understanding
2. exposure to fields of study and occupations
3. stimulation to pursue higher level goals

Ann Dirkes (1977) has shown that creative thinking techniques can be used to teach basic skills and concepts in mathematics. De Vito and Krockover (1976) presented models for use of creativity in science. Our own research

(Feldhusen, Bahlke & Treffinger, 1969) indicated that through the teaching of creative thinking, children also made substantial gains in language skills.

Recent developmental work (Feldhusen & Kolloff, 1979; OrRico & Feldhusen, 1979) indicated that instruction in creative thinking and problem solving within the context of the three-stage model can be used to help gifted students learn about fields of study and higher level careers. The results of yet another project (Moore, Feldhusen & Owings, 1978) indicate that such career education activity stimulates gifted students to plan and strive for higher level educational and occupational goals.

Thus, we conclude that instruction in creative thinking and problem solving is fundamental in enrichment programs for the gifted. Some advocates of gifted programs argue that the sole and primary ingredient is acceleration. We have no quarrel with the need to accelerate instruction for the gifted, if that means something more than simply offering instruction earlier than usual. For the gifted acceleration ought to include larger amounts of information presented faster and earlier than the normal curriculum, increased abstraction in teaching, higher level verbal processing in reading and writing, and above all challenging instruction which stimulates the gifted to strive for mastery and understanding. In sum, acceleration should include early introduction to the tools of both convergent and divergent thinking as well as evaluation. Our major purpose of this chapter has been to argue for the crucial role of divergent or creative thinking and problem solving in instruction for the gifted.

A Model for Enrichment Programs

There was a time when enrichment for the gifted meant instruction carried out by the regular teacher for a gifted child in the regular classroom. Martinson (1972) concluded that such efforts to enrich instruction in the regular classroom were generally unsuccessful.

As described briefly earlier in this chapter, Feldhusen and Kolloff (1978) developed a creative enrichment model which stresses the development of basic thinking skills, cognitive strategies, and independent learning in gifted children. This model will be described next in greater detail. Instruction in this model is supplementary to the regular curriculum and may include reading, language skill activity, mathematics, social studies, science and art, but all are proferred as supplements to the regular curriculum. The gifted students meet in small groups of six to twelve and pursue three kinds of activities (Feldhusen & Kolloff, 1978). It has also been adapted successfully to career education (OrRico & Feldhusen, 1979).

Stage one activities in the model are designed to teach and strengthen basic divergent, convergent, and imagination abilities and to foster basic language and mathematic skills. Activities at this level are selected and directed by the teacher. They are generally short term in nature requiring 15 to 30 minutes for a lesson. Good illustrations of divergent thinking and language arts skills are found in Renzulli and Callahan's *New Directions in Creativity* (1973). A fluency activity requires children to list things which are soft and blue. A language activity calls for antonyms and synonyms for given words. Excellent examples of convergent thinking skills are found in Harnadek's *Deductive Thinking Skills* (1978) and mathematics in Siegel and Wiseman's *Visual Thinking Skills for Reading and Math* (1978). Stage one activities can be seeded throughout the program. Information transmission via reading and listening is also a basic activity related to stage one. These activities are guided by specific objectives and are designed to foster basic skills and abilities in divergent and convergent thinking.

Stage two is concerned with fostering broader strategies using convergent, divergent, evaluative, and cognition skills. The gifted students assume somewhat more self direction in these activities, but the teacher is still basically the selector and director. There are many examples of this type of activity in Renzulli and Callahan's *New Directions in Creativity* (1973). Creating a new product, planning an advertising campaign, designing product packages, doing the layout for a space ship or writing a script are illustrations of this stage activities. Similarly teaching the creative problem solving model, synectics, morphological analysis, or logical analysis of arguments in a story are illustrations of these stage two strategies. The emphasis is on the teaching of broader and more practical cognitive skills and strategies. These activities are often longer in duration ranging from one to several hours and spreading over several days or weeks.

Stage three introduces gifted students to independent project activity in which they can use their basic skills and abilities, information acquired through reading and listening, and cognitive strategies taught in stage two to develop facility in self direction in larger and more realistic projects. The students explore their own experiential background and interests in defining projects. Motivation must be increasingly internal. Creativity is stressed. The teacher now assumes the resource role. The student plans and conducts his/ her own investigation, inquiry, or project. The goal is to develop increased capacity for such self direction, self motivation and use of creative skills.

Stage three activities come to predominate in the model as children make progress in stage one and two. It is assumed that gifted children will spend two to six hours a week in some administrative arrangement for the three-stage program. The time working with a teacher might occur during the school day, after school or Saturdays. Typically there is outside or home work carried on by the student when not in session with a teacher. The work or project activity may grow out of each of the basic curricular areas, mathematics, science, language arts and social studies. A sound program also offers continuing guidance in reading both in supplementary literature and in books related to project activity.

Who teaches this enrichment program? There are many alternatives. Some cost money, others do not. It is very helpful to have a paid special gifted resource teacher. Such a teacher can be trained intensively and can travel from school to school serving the programs in several locations. Resource teachers can also be hired part-time or combined with some other specialty such as a coordinator in a curricular area such as language arts. Other alternatives involve hiring unemployed teachers on an hourly basis, hiring parents who have college education, or recruiting others from the community who have expertise for the programs.

Some approaches require no special budget. In some schools the librarian meets with small gifted groups while an aide tends the library. Parent volunteers or community resource people can often be recruited without pay. Teacher volunteers may work with the gifted after school. Occasionally the teachers at a grade level organize themselves departmentally and free one of the team to work with the gifted a certain amount of time each week. Many alternatives are possible.

The program described here serves the needs of children who are moderately advanced in the basic curricular areas or creatively gifted. Those who are highly advanced in one or more areas should also be given some form of acceleration. Figure 2.1 shows various forms of acceleration which can be used across the K–12 spectrum. Achievement tests given as a part of the regular school testing program can be used to identify very high achievers (95% ile in math, or reading, or language skills). However, standardized achievement tests often fail to tap the true level of achievement of a gifted child because too low a form of the test is used in relation to grade placement. A gifted child in grade two taking a test for levels 1–3 would not have sufficient challenge to assess his/her highest potential level of performance. Children who are seen as possibly gifted should be tested with higher level forms of the test.

Research indicates (Getzels & Dillon, 1973) that acceleration is effective in improving achievement of gifted students. The major forms as shown in Figure 2.1 are early admission to school, grade advancement, special accelerated classes, college courses in high school, and early admission to college. All can be used successfully to accelerate educational programs for gifted children who are very high achievers in one or more areas of the curriculum.

Individualized Educational Programs (IEP) for the Gifted

Enrichment activities for gifted students in the regular classroom seemed not to produce measurable gains or advantages according to research cited earlier. However, new efforts to individualize and specify learning outcomes for the gifted show promise of overcoming the failures of general enrichment programs. Perhaps it is the required specificity of a learning contract as well as the learning objectives, both of which often characterize this approach, which may make the difference.

Feldhusen, Rand and Crowe (1975) described a system for individualizing instruction based on use of learning agreements and learning centers. The system individualizes instruction in several basic skills areas and classroom art activities. Children plan by the day or week according to activities which are listed on a chart as available. They can create their own order or sequence, proceed at their own rates, and emphasize certain areas over others. The system is uniquely successful with gifted children who have heightened capacity to read and learn independently. Gifted children can forge ahead in basic skills areas and in conceptual learning to higher levels appropriate to their abilities. The teacher watches each child's plan very carefully, urges modification to include more time on basic skills if necessary, and evaluates each child's progress. The teacher also meets with small groups for reading and project activities and with the whole class for some activities such as social studies, book reports and class discussions.

Another individualized approach is Project UP (Unlimited Potential; Marion Community Schools, 1978). Students are identified by classroom teachers utilizing checklists for four areas: learning ability, motivation, leadership, and creativity. One resource teacher is needed at the elementary level and one at the secondary level to assist teachers in the identification process and in other activities to be described next. Project UP provides the checklist forms for identification.

Once the child has been identified as gifted a conference is arranged with the parents to explain the programs and to secure more information about the child. The child is also interviewed to assess his/her interests and to explain the program. Forms are provided for these interviews.

Each student then plans activities with assistance from the teacher and following lists of suggestions provided by Project UP. General suggestions are provided for activities, although they are sometimes quite vague. For example:

> Providing activities that cover a range of difficulty and the scope of complexity as they relate to a particular area or skill

> or

> Affording students with opportunities to avail themselves of expertise in the community

It is doubtful that such extremely vague statements would be of value to teachers; hopefully the resource teachers would have more concrete suggestions for activities.

Once an activity has been formulated a written statement is prepared and signed as a contract or agreement by the student, teacher, and parent.

Once a project is completed, the teacher evaluates it and prepares a written report. The Project UP manual gives a list of reading and study resources and spells out the roles of the parents, teacher, and student quite precisely. This project offers one quite good framework for developing individual plans and activities for the gifted.

Treffinger (1979a) offered specific recommendations for schools which are planning IEPs for gifted, creative and talented students.

1. Attention should be given to the unique talents and characteristics of each student using information from the cumulative folder and from the identification process.
2. The IEP should take into account the student's interests, motivation, and learning style.
3. The IEP goals should focus on basic skill learning, enrichment activities, acceleration when appropriate, fostering independence and self direction, experience in valuing, and personal development.
4. IEPs for the gifted should often explore the unknown and futuristic concerns.
5. There should be much experience in finding and solving problems, inquiry skills, and research methodology.
6. Gifted students should participate in the development of the IEP.
7. The IEP should provide for coordination of learning resources at school, at home, and in the community.
8. The IEP should serve to facilitate communication among the student, teacher, parents, and community resource persons regarding the student's program.
9. IEPs should be continuously monitored by the student, teacher, and parents and adapted as necessary.
10. There should be a good system of evaluation and record keeping with both students and teachers participating in the evaluation process.

These guidelines can provide excellent direction for schools which are developing individualized programs for the gifted. It is often the case that teachers may wish to use IEPs not only with gifted, creative, and talented students but also with the whole class. This may be potentially constructive, although caution must be exercised to minimize the possibility that the gifted, creative and talented will be "lost in the shuffle" and will engage in activities not really different from those pursued by less able peers. If the IEPs are to be used with the whole class we urge careful consideration of the model described by Feldhusen, Rand, and Crowe (1975). It affords a proven system for implementing all the guidelines offered by Treffinger (1979a) If the IEPs are to be used only with the gifted, creative and talented, Project UP (Marion Public Schools, 1978) affords a practical model. However, the latter project offers little or no guidance concerning learning activities. For more specific direction to appropriate activities, the model described by Feldhusen and Kolloff 1978, 1979 and by OrRico and Feldhusen 1979 and Feldhusen, Hynes and Richardson (1977) offer concrete guidelines for the teacher. Guidance for effective planning of individualized instructional materials may be found in Treffinger, Hohn, and Feldhusen (1979). An additional model for developing IEPs for gifted and talented students is presented by Renzulli and Smith (1979).

Summary

This chapter focussed on methods and activities for teaching creative thinking and problem solving to gifted, creative and talented students. We have described several approaches, models, and systems which have been implemented with groups and individual gifted students. The authors are currently conducting numerous programs for gifted children in classrooms. Programs can be developed to meet the individual needs of students by effectively using the resources of the teachers and the community.

REFERENCES

De Vito, A., & Krockover, G.H. *Creative Sciencing.* Boston: Little, Brown, 1976.

Dirkes, A.M. Learning through creative thinking. *Gifted Child Quarterly,* 1977, *21,* 526–537.

Feldhusen, J.F., Bahlke, S.J., and Treffinger, D.J. Teaching creative thinking. *Elementary School Journal,* 1969, *70,* 48–53.

Feldhusen, J.F., Rand, D., and Crowe, M. Designing open and individualized instruction at the elementary level. *Educational Technology,* 1975, 15, 17–21.

Feldhusen, J.F., Hynes, K.P., and Richardson, W.D. Curriculum materials for vocational organizations. *Clearing House,* 1977, *50,* 224–226.

Feldhusen, J.F., and Kolloff, M.B. A three-stage model for gifted education. *G/C/T,* 1978, *1,* 3–5 and 53–58.

Feldhusen, J.F., and Kolloff, M.B. A rationale for career education activities in the Purdue three-stage enrichment model for gifted education. *Roeper Review,* 1979, *2,* 13–17.

Getzels, J.W., and Dillon, J.T. The nature of giftedness and the education of the gifted. In R.M.W. Travers (Ed.) *Second Handbook of Research on Teaching.* Chicago: Rand McNally, 1973, 689–731.

Goertzel, M.G., Goertzel, V., and Goertzel, T.G. *Three Hundred Eminent Personalities.* San Francisco: Jossey-Bass, 1978.

Harnadek, A. *Deductive Thinking Skills.* Troy, Michigan: Midwest Publications, 1978.

Marion Community Schools (Indiana). *Project UP, Guidelines for Elementary Teachers.* Marion, Indiana: Marion Schools, 1978.

Martinson, R.A. Research on the gifted and talented: Its implications for education. In S.P. Marland (Ed.) *Education of the Gifted and Talented, Volume 2.* Background Papers submitted to the U.S. Office of Education. Washington, D.C.: U.S. Government Printing Office, 1971, A–1 to A–79.

Moore, B.A., Feldhusen, J.F., and Owings, J. *The Professional Career Exploration Program for Minority and/or Low Income Gifted and Talented High School Students*. West Lafayette, Indiana: Purdue University Department of Education, 1978.

Noller, R.B. *Scratching the Surface of Creative Problem-Solving: A Bird's Eye View of CPS*. Buffalo: DOK, 1977.

Noller, R.B., Treffinger, D.J., and Houseman, E.D. *It's a Gas to be Gifted: CPS for the Gifted & Talented*. Buffalo: DOK, 1979.

OrRico, M.J., and Feldhusen, J.F. Career education for the gifted and talented: Some problems and solutions. *G/C/T,* Nov.–Dec., 1979.

Parnes, S.J. *Creative Behavior Guidebook*. New York: Charles Scribners, 1967.

Parnes, S.J., Noller, R.B., and Biondi, A.M. *Guide to Creative Action*. New York: Charles Scribner, 1977.

Renzulli, J.S., and Callahan, C.M. *New Directions in Creativity*. New York: Harper & Row, 1973.

Renzulli, J.S. *The Enrichment Triad Model*. Mansfield Center, Connecticut: Creative Learning Press, 1977.

Renzulli, J.S., and Smith, L.H. *Developing Individual Educational Programs (IEPs) for the Gifted and Talented*. Mansfield Center, Connecticut: Creative Learning Press, 1979.

Siegel, K., and Wiseman, R. *Visual Thinking Skills for Reading and Math*. Troy, Michigan: Midwest Publications, 1978.

Starkweather, E.K. Creativity research instruments designed for use with preschool children. *Journal of Creative Behavior,* 1971, 5, 245–255.

Treffinger, D.J. Individual educational plans for gifted, talented and creative students. In: Butterfield, S., and others. *IEPS for the Gifted and Talented*. Ventura, California: Ventura County Superintendent of Schools, LTI Publications, 1979 (a).

Treffinger, D.J. *Encouraging Creative Learning for the Gifted and Talented*. Ventura, CA: Ventura County Schools, LTI Publications, 1979b.

Treffinger, D.J., Hohn, R.L., and Feldhusen, J.F. *Reach Each You Teach*. Buffalo: DOK, 1979.

Treffinger, D.J., and Barton, B.L. Fostering independent learning. *G/C/T,* March-April 1979.

Treffinger, D.J., and Barton, B.L. *Encouraging Self-Directed Learning*. Mansfield Center, Connecticut: Creative Learning Press, 1980.

Chapter 3

SPECIAL NEEDS OF MINORITY AND DISADVANTAGED GIFTED STUDENTS

There is an urgent need to improve instruction in creative problem solving especially for disadvantaged gifted students. The many pressing social, political, and technological problems which face our nation and our world will best be solved by citizens who have become good thinkers. Creative problem solving is the major and essential ingredient of effective thinking. One purpose of this book, therefore, is to present, describe, and discuss promising methods, programs or sets of instructional materials for teaching creative problem solving to disadvantaged students. In addition to providing detailed information about instructional materials, there are also suggestions to teachers to guide them in developing new creative problem solving activities as demonstration projects. Our ultimate purpose is to stimulate more teachers of the disadvantaged to introduce instruction for creative problem solving in their classes.

While "teaching for thinking" has been a commonly stated goal in American education, there is substantial evidence that it has not been widely achieved by our schools. Educators have observed the discrepancy between our goals and actual school practices. Many critics of education reached similar conclusions, but apparently have not stimulated any widespread change in classroom behavior. As the world is confronted by an increasing number of critical problems, and students become increasingly sensitive to the need to be educated to solve them, more and more pressures are brought to bear on teachers and school administrators. Intensive efforts are needed to provide teacher, administrators, and students with the skills, resources, and information that are needed to broaden the range of instructional activities. The need for such efforts is dramatically underscored when specific consideration is given to disadvantaged segments of our population.

Disadvantaged Students Need Creative Problem Solving Skills

Children from some disadvantaged families face severe handicaps at home and in school in their cognitive development. Effective thinking, creativity, and problem solving are neither valued highly, nor adequately modeled in the home, and many teachers lack skill in developing these abilities among students in the schools.

Our definition of disadvantaged children refers to youngsters who have suffered some deficit in their cognitive development due to socioeconomic and/ or ethnic background factors in their homes, schools, and communities. Cicirelli (1972) described three models which attempt to explain the causes of student deficit. Of these models the most appropriate for the point of view of this book is the environment deficit model. This model asserts that the failure of the disadvantaged to achieve results from a lack of stimulation in the environment. Other deficit models Cicirelli describes are the genetic deficit model and the nutritional deficit model. The genetic deficit model argues that differences in intelligence are hereditary and that environmental manipulation can do little to improve school achievement for the disadvantaged. The nutritional deficit model suggests that lack of school achievement by the disadvantaged may be the result of inadequate prenatal or early childhood nutrition which affects brain development and general health.

There are two other broad viewpoints of the disadvantaged which emphasize school disparity and deactualization (Cicirelli, 1972). The school disparity model views students as well equipped to learn if the schools would choose the proper methods to teach them. Those who adhere to this model suggest that a cultural difference exists between the disadvantaged student and the middle class school. Others suggest that disadvantaged students have basic attitudes and values which have been learned in a culture of poverty. These values are very different from values held by American mainstream culture. Some have suggested that the cognitive deficit exhibited by disadvantaged Americans is due solely to teachers' and administrators' prejudice against children of the poor and their expectations that such students will not be able to achieve.

The third view of the disadvantaged suggests that the underachieving student is one who has not been motivated or given the opportunity to actualize his/her potential. This deactualization model, based on a humanistic view of the individual as unique and basically good, suggests that individuals are motivated to develop their fullest potential in relation to their own goals and values.

Another approach to describing and classifying the barriers which must be overcome by disadvantaged gifted students has been described by Baldwin, Gear, and Lucito (1978). They describe a model in which three different sets of obstacles or barriers, singly or in various combinations, may inhibit the recognition or development of outstanding talents. These are: *socioeconomic deprivation, cultural diversity,* and *geographic isolation.* In order to assist disadvantaged students in developing their full potential, it is necessary to determine the degree to which these barriers may be influencing the student's work and motivation, and to be able to plan an appropriate response. Of course, different responses may be required according to which factors, or combination of factors, are relevant for particular students. The model thus points out the importance of investigating the *specific* dimensions of disadvantage, rather than making overly general assumptions about disadvantaged students as if they were a single, homogeneous group.

Creative Problem Solving for the Disadvantaged

Despite the fact that teaching pupils to think creatively and to solve problems are central goals of education, American schools have failed to a large extent to provide appropriate instruction; this problem seems especially critical for disadvantaged students. While some problem-solving activities are found in most science and mathematics curricula, and in some social studies programs, they tend to follow narrowly-prescribed traditional modes of inquiry, and frequently involve trivial problems. Furthermore, even these simple attempts are often not included in the curriculum in inner city schools.

Many of the characteristics which teachers appear to value most highly, and so to cultivate in their classrooms, may be inimical to the improvement of creative thinking and problem-solving abilities among disadvantaged students. Torrance observed:

> . . . teachers and parents give evidence of being more concerned about having "good children," in the sense of their being easy to manage, well-behaved, and adjusted to social norms. It is rare that we are genuinely willing for a child to achieve his potentialities (1965, p. 14).

The problem of developing "good" or well-behaved children as opposed to teaching students to become more creative thinkers and better problem solvers is particularly acute in inner-city schools. Teachers in these schools are very much concerned with discipline and "good behavior." Frequently, such behavior is emphasized at the expense of more appropriate cognitive goals.

There are also indications that many of the skills and cognitive abilities which are stressed in school are likely to result in further handicaps for disadvantaged students. Many studies have shown that disadvantaged students often perform poorly on the measures of achievement, intelligence, and cognitive development which are predominantly used in public school settings (Bloom, Davis, and Hess, 1965; Deutsch, Katz, and Jensen, 1968; Frost and Hawks, 1966; Kennedy, Van DeRiet, and White, 1963).

Examples of areas in which disadvantaged students have been found to be limited, which may also be importantly related to the development of problem-solving, creative-thinking, and other complex-cognitive abilities, include: verbal skills and symbolic representation (Vairo and Whittaker, 1967; Blank and Soloman, 1969; John, 1963; John and Goldstein, 1967); abstract thinking and flexibility (Roberts, 1967; Hirsch, 1969; Jensen, 1968); general reading abilities (Stauffer, 1967); and problem solving (Feldhusen, et al., 1972; Houtz and Feldhusen, 1975).

Recent research has been directed towards the identification of strengths of disadvantaged students. Torrance (1973) developed a checklist to assist in the identification of creatively gifted disadvantaged children. This checklist presents a variety of behaviors that may be observed when children are actively engaged in classroom activities. The behaviors reflect strengths and abilities which can be developed through appropriate instruction.

Often, disadvantaged students' classrooms include instructions, books or problems which are too abstract or meaningless for them. Instead, they need first to understand concepts on a "personal" level, by working with those things with which they are most familiar.

Students must learn to determine differences between relevant and irrelevent information, to make hypotheses, and to evaluate their ideas. Bruce (1967) asserts that these aspects of problem solving are neglected in schools. Although texts may show how others have sought answers to their questions, disadvantaged students need to be active participants in solving problems which are relevant to them in order to develop these cognitive processes. Jarvis (1965) stressed the need for disadvantaged elementary school students to be explicitly taught the intellectual operations of critical thinking, rather than teaching them what to think, or expecting that they will learn these operations as a by-product of their classroom studies.

Instead, teachers should introduce problem-solving instruction, and through this instruction develop the material (Jarvis, 1965). Kelson (1968) suggested that the curriculum should include materials built around real or relevant problems. Using such materials, knowledge and skills could be introduced as needed. There would be no need to teach discipline-oriented knowledge simply because it might be useful later.

Dawson (1970) called for learning situations which would interest the students, relate to their daily lives, and involve them in the learning process. Dawson found that role playing with realistic problem situations can be used to encourage the students to engage in planning, imaginative thinking, problem solving, and discussion. He concluded that students not only learned by handling relevant problems through acting them out, but also learned to take and give criticism.

Torrance (1974) recently suggested that planning for and thinking about the future be used as vehicles in developing children's creative thinking and problem-solving abilities:

> Schools are accustomed to teaching to deepen children's understanding of a present event by helping them learn about its history. It is just as important to help them speculate knowledgeably about the event's future (p. 65).

Disadvantaged students can use their positive strengths and abilities in oral expression, movement, and acting as well as in discussion, writing, and creative art to tackle the problems of the future. Hopefully such experience will better equip them to deal with present problems.

Ross (1968) asserted that there are no disadvantaged students in art, since all students have feelings and can express them. Techniques were described to help students become more aware of their environment. By having them photograph various scenes around the city they began to see the environment in a new way and tried to shape it artistically. By doing this, Ross argued, they could develop insights and perceptions necessary to reshape the environment in later years. This assignment also had other influences. The students were able to question (and try to answer) what their place was in the environment. The photographs and paintings helped compare objective reality to a subjective record thereby offering them a better view of the world. The creative study of their environment may also have produced some parallel growth in other areas. The students seemed to be more motivated to read, to gain more information on the subjects photographed, and to write about their creations.

Torrance (1969) proposed that developing the potential of disadvantaged students is possible, but that our efforts have been limited by our failure to identify and develop the talents which are valued by particular subcultures. Torrance identified a set of "creative positives," which he concluded occur among disadvantaged children with high frequency, and upon which programs for the development of talent might successfully be created. These "creative positives" were: high nonverbal fluency and originality; high creative productivity in small groups; adeptness in visual art activities; high creativity in movement, dance, and other physical activities, high motivation for games, music, sports, humor, and concrete objects; and rich imagery in language. Torrance (1969, 76–77) also described characteristics of school programs for disadvantaged students which have attempted to provide opportunities for talent development (Witt, 1968; Howe, 1969; Bruch, 1969).

Torrance (1971) reviewed studies of differential performance of racial groups and socioeconomic class comparisons on measures of creative thinking in a wide variety of geographical areas. In reviewing more than a dozen studies, Torrance noted that in relation to verbal creative-thinking abilities, most studies reported either superior performance by advantaged pupils, or no significant differences. In many studies of nonverbal creative-thinking abilities, however, disadvantaged students scored as well or better than more advantaged groups. Torrance concluded that the creative potential of disadvantaged students must be respected and developed in school and community programs. Such emphases may be as important as or even more important than emphases on compensation of deficits.

Approaches to Training

It seems there are many different ways for teachers who recognize the importance of creativity and problem solving to bring training in these areas into their classrooms. Teachers can also plan ways to use this training in subject areas already in the curriculum. However, teachers need to have a better understanding of creative problem solving before they can present it to their students (Jarvis, 1965). Above all, the problem of providing training which may be too abstract, and therefore irrelevant and confusing for the child, must be avoided.

Disadvantaged students are greatly influenced by the environment in which they live. Their homes and school experiences may affect them in such a way as to hinder their growth in concept formation, verbal proficiency, and transition from concrete to abstract thought. These areas are more important in the development of problem-solving abilities.

A number of programs and sets of instructional material are now available for teaching creative problem solving. While it seems that creative and energetic teachers can do much to develop and use their own materials and methods for teaching creative problem solving, hopefully systematically developed and evaluated materials could make the teacher's task easier or could help teachers do a better job.

Disadvantaged and Minority Gifted

There has been much new attention focussed on identifying and nurturing giftedness, talent and creativity among minorities and the disadvantaged during the last decade. With a grant from the U.S. Office of Education's Office of Career Education, Moore, Owings and Feldhusen (1979) carried out an extensive project in four high schools developing techniques for the identification and nurturance of giftedness, and creativity among students from minority and economically disadvantaged families. They used Torrance's (1969) *Checklist of Creative Positives,* a teacher rating scale designed for use with minority children, several scales from Renzulli's (1975) *Scales for Rating the Behaviorial Characteristics of Superior Students,* also teacher rating scales, group IQ tests, standardized achievement test results, student essays and interviews and a screening committee to seek out students for a Professional Careers Exploration Program. Students studied professional and other high level careers in the classroom and experienced several occupations with job site mentors. An intensive evaluation showed the program to be successful in its goals to identify these gifted students and provide career exploration experience. Of special significance is the fact that some of the gifted students in this project had IQs as low as 108. However, other signs of ability from the Torrance Checklist of Creative Positives and the Renzulli Scales showed them to be truly gifted.

Moore (1978), the Director of the Professional Career Exploration Program, in emphasizing the dual need for career education for the gifted and the need for special programs for minority and disadvantaged students stated the case as follows:

> Our country cannot afford to overlook the professional areas and the human resources of the gifted and talented, minority and/or low income students. In particular, these future leaders should have the opportunity to select the most satisfying and challenging career regardless of past cultural or socioeconomic disadvantages (pp. 336–337).

Bruch (1978) reviewed the literature in the area of education of the culturally different gifted. She concluded that there is a special need to develop new programs for the culturally different gifted with input from both the dominant culture and the minority culture. Both groups should be involved in such program development. She states that:

> The gifted in each culture could be the significant leaders in learning to deal with problem solving the issues of cultural pluralism. Inter-ethnic understanding in a particular locale could be expanded to learning vicariously about less accessible cultural groups. Brighter youngsters would be expected to reject cultural stereotypes (pp. 376–377).

Torrance (1978) reviewed developments in identification and teaching minority and disadvantaged gifted students and concluded that modest gains have been made. He reviewed his own extensive work in this area and various other projects throughout the United States. His own work clearly indicates that creativity is an important strength in minority and disadvantaged gifted students and that creative characteristics can be used as a basis for identification of minority and disadvantaged gifted students. He also argues that creativity and problem solving provide excellent ways of developing instruction for these gifted students.

Conclusion

It seems clear that the gifted, creative and talented are well represented among youth from minority and disadvantaged family backgrounds, that with special efforts and methods they can be identified, and that creativity and problem solving provide bases for developing sound educational programs to meet their needs.

REFERENCES

Baldwin, A.Y., Gear, G., and Lucito, L. *Educational planning for the gifted: Overcoming cultural, geographic, and socioeconomic barriers.* Reston, VA: Council for Exceptional Children, 1978.

Blank, M., and Soloman, F. How shall the disadvantaged child be taught? *Child Development,* 1969, 40, 47–61.

Bloom, B.D., Davis, A., and Hess, R. *Compensatory Education for Cultural Deprivation.* New York: Holt, Rinehart and Winston, 1965.

Bruce, R.J. A review of textbook materials. In B.C. Cox and B.G. Massialas (eds.) *Social Studies in the United States.* New York: Harcourt, Brace, and World, 1967.

Bruch, C.B. *A proposed rational for the identification and development of the gifted disadvantaged.* Athens, Georgia: University of Georgia, Department of Educational Psychology, 1969.

Bruch, C.B. Recent insights on culturally different gifted. *Gifted Child Quarterly,* 1978, 22, 374–393.

Cicerelli, V.G. Educational models for the disadvantaged. In Walberg, H.S. and Kapan, A.T. (eds) *Rethinking Urban Education.* San Francisco: Jossey-Bass, 1972, 31–48.

Dawson, H.S. *On the Outskirts of Hope.* New York: McGraw-Hill, 1970.

Duetsch, M., Katz, I., and Jensen, A.R. (eds) *Social Class, Race, and Psychological Development.* New York: Holt, Rinehart, and Winston, 1968.

Feldhusen, J.F., Houtz, J.C., and Ringenbach, S. The Purdue Elementary Problem Solving Inventory. *Psychological Reports,* 1972, 31, 891–901.

Frost, J.L. and Hawkes, G.R. (eds) *The Disadvantaged Children-Issues and Innovations.* New York: Houghton Mifflin, 1966.

Hirsch, J.G. Individual characteristics and academic achievement. In J.M. Beck and R.W. Saxe (eds) *Teaching and the Culturally Disadvantaged Pupil.* Springfield, Illinois: Charles Thomas, 1969.

Houtz, J.C. and Feldhusen, J.F. Problem solving ability of disadvantaged elementary school children under four testing formats: A replicated experiment. *Psychology in the Schools,* 1975, 12, 26–33.

Howe, F. Untaught teachers and improbable poets. Saturday Review. March 1969, 52, 60–2.

Jarvis, O.T. Thinking and classroom problem solving. *Education,* 1965, 86, 111–116.

Jensen, A.R. How much can we boost IQ and scholastic achievement? *Harvard Educational Review,* 1968 (Winter), 39, 1–123.

John, V.P. and Goldstein, L.S. The social context of language acquisition. In M. Deutsch (eds) *The Disadvantage Child.* New York: Basic, 1967.

Kelson, K.R. New curricular materials and the teaching of the disadvantaged. Address given to the NDEA National Institute Conference, Project Report: I. July, 1968.

Kennedy, W.A., Van deRiet, V., and White, J.C. Jr. A normative sample of intelligence and achievement of Negro elementary school children in the Southeastern United States, *Monographs of the Society for Research in Child Development,* 1963, 28 (6 Serial No. 90).

Moore, B.A. Career education for disadvantaged gifted high school students. *Gifted Child Quarterly,* 1978, 22, 332–337.

Moore, B.A., Feldhusen, J.F. & Owings, J. *The Professional Career Exploration Program for Minority and/or Low Income Gifted and Talented High School Students.* West Lafayette, Indiana: Purdue University, 1978.

Renzulli, J.S., Hartman, R.K., and Callahan, C.M. Scale for Rating The Behavioral Characteristics of Superior Students. In Barbe, W.B. and Renzulli, J.S. (eds) *Psychology and Education of the Gifted.* New York: Halsted Press, 1975, 264–273.

Roberts, J.I. (ed) *School Children in the Urban Slum.* New York: Free Press, 1967.

Ross, J. The relationship of simple audiovisual techniques to the arts and the disadvantaged. *Audiovisual Instructor,* 1968, 13, 44–45.

Stauffer, R.G. (ed) The *First-grade Studies: Findings of Individual Investigations.* Newark, Delaware: International Reading Association, 1967.

Torrance, E.P. Creative positives of disadvantaged children and youth. *Gifted Child Quarterly,* 1969, 13, 71–81.

————. Are the Torrance Tests of Creative Thinking biased against or in favor of "disadvantaged" groups? *Gifted Child Quarterly,* 1971, 15, 75–80.

————. Nontest indicators of creative talent among disadvantaged children. *Gifted Child Quarterly,* 1973, 17, 3–9.

————. Ways gifted children can study the future. *The Gifted Child Quarterly,* 1974, 18, 65–71.

Torrance, E.P. Dare we hope again? *Gifted Child Quarterly,* 1978, 22, 292–312.

Vairo, P.D. and Whittaker, F. Needed learning tools for the deprived child. *Peabody Journal of Education,* 1967, 45, 121–123.

Witt, G. *The Life Enrichment Activity Program: A Brief History.* New Haven: LEAP Inc., 1968.

SUPPLEMENTARY BIBLIOGRAPHY ON THE CULTURALLY DIFFERENT GIFTED

Adler, S. Data gathering: The reliability and validity of test data from culturally different children. *Journal of Learning Disabilities,* 1973, 6(7), 430–434.

Ames, L.B. Academic promise in Negro primary school pupils. *Journal of Disabilities,* 1968, 1(10), 16–22.

Bernal, E.M. Jr. Gifted programs for the culturally different. NASSP Bulletin. 1976, 60(398), 67–76.

Brazzil, W.F. Higher horizons in southern elementary schools. *Journal of Negro Education,* 1964, 33, 382–389.

Bruch, C.B. Modification of procedures for identification of the disadvantaged gifted. *Gifted Child Quarterly,* 1971, 15(4), 267–272.

Bruch, C.B. Assessment of creativity in culturally different children. *Gifted Child Quarterly,* 1976, 19(2), 164 174.

Cox, J.A. Suggested instruments for the identification of the preschool and kindergarten disadvantaged gifted. *Southern Journal of Educational Research,* 1974, 8(5), 198–208(10).

Davis, T. and Pyatskowit, A. Bicognitive education: A new future for the Indian child? *Journal of American Indian Education,* 1976, 15(3), 14–21.

Fitzgibbons, C.T. Identification of mentally gifted "disadvantaged" students at the eight grade level. *Journal of Negro Education,* 1975, 43(1), 53–66.

Gallagher, J.J. The culturally different gifted. In J.J. Gallagher's *Teaching the gifted child,* Boston: Allyn and Bacon, 1975, 366–387.

Gowan, J.C. Issues in the education of disadvantaged gifted children. *Gifted Child Quarterly,* 1968, 12, 115–119.

Hampton, P.J. Talent among disadvantaged students. *Educational Forum,* 1974, 38(3), 321–326.

Lynn, B. Disadvantaged gifted—A residential school. *Gifted Child Quarterly,* 1968, 12(1), 18–22.

Meeker, M.N. and Meeker, R. Strategies for assessing intellectual patterns in Black, Anglo, and Mexican-American boys—or any other children—and implications for education, *Journal of School Psychology,* 1973, 11(4), 341–350.

Passow, A.H. The gifted and the disadvantaged. *National Elementary Principal.* 1972, 51(5), 24–31.

Renzulli, J.S. The potential for creativity among minority groups. *Education Review,* 1969, *7,* 59–62.

Renzulli, J.S. The identification and development of talent potential among the disadvantaged. *Contemporary Education,* 1971, *42*(3), 122–125.

Sato, I.S. The culturally different gifted child—The dawning of his day? *Exceptional Children,* 1974, *40*(8), 572–576.

Soloman, A.O. Analysis of creative thinking of disadvantaged children. *Journal of Creative Behavior,* 1975, *8*(4), 293–295.

Taylor, C.W. Cultivating new talents: A way to reach the educationally deprived. *Journal of Creative Behavior, 1968, 2*(2), 83–90.

Torrance, E.P. Assessment of disadvantaged minority group children. *School Psychology Digest,* 1973, *2*(4), 3–10.

Chapter 4

METHODS OF TEACHING CREATIVITY AND PROBLEM SOLVING

You should not be content to wait for creativity and problem solving to occur "spontaneously" in teaching the gifted. If you really want to emphasize goals that involve fostering these thinking processes, it will be necessary for you to take some very direct, deliberate action to see that it happens!

In this chapter, we shall review some of the methods and techniques that you can use in your classroom to stimulate creative thinking and problem solving. They are not "tricks" or "games" that are ends in themselves, of course, and they can be utilized as you are carrying out your regular, day-to-day instruction in language arts, social studies, or almost any other subject area.

Each of the sections of this chapter will deal with an aspect of the problem that has been widely-studied and written about. Our purpose is not to provide a detailed explanation and scholarly criticism of the method, but merely to provide you with an introduction to illustrate some useful techniques that can be applied by any teacher working with gifted students.

Fostering a Creative Classroom Climate

Creativity can be viewed as a process of change in thinking and action. The combination of ideas previously unconnected into a novel idea or concept requires change. In order to foster creativity in your classroom, it is necessary to create an atmosphere that is receptive to new ideas. A positive, reinforcing, accepting climate is the basic ingredient necessary for the nurturance of creative behavior. Many obstacles to creative thinking are emotional reactions to insecure feelings which are caused by fear of new or different ideas. By suggesting novel ideas people open themselves to criticism. It is often easier to conform to the norm than risk making a fool of oneself by expressing a novel idea or thought. New or different ideas can flourish in an open system, one that is flexible and oriented towards the individual student. In such an atmosphere, the emphasis rests on the student's interests and ideas. This can be accomplished by creating a climate of mutual respect and acceptance between students and teacher.

It is sometimes difficult to be creative because of learned attitudes. These attitudes are often expressed by statements such as "I have a mental block against math" or "I'm not very good at solving puzzles." Blocks in thought patterns which inhibit creative thinking may be caused by perception or emotion.

By encouraging and reinforcing unusual ideas, students' attitudes can be positively directed towards a willingness to think and experiment with new ideas. Continued support and positive attitudes from the teacher are the fuel necessary to power the positive motivational climate that will set the stage for a creative atmosphere. An environment of adaptation to individual pupil's needs and interests, willingness to modify and vary planned activities in the interest and support of the students, and emphasis on divergent thinking skills will result in a warm and spontaneous climate which will spawn creativity in delightful dimensions.

Here are some general suggestions for creating an atmosphere conducive to creative thinking:

1. Support and reinforce unusual ideas and responses of students.
2. Use failure as a positive to help students realize errors and meet acceptable standards in a supportive atmosphere.
3. Adapt to student interests and ideas in the classroom whenever possible.
4. Allow time for students to think about and develop their creative ideas. Not all creativity occurs immediately and spontaneously.
5. Create a climate of mutual respect and acceptance between students and between students and teachers, so that students can share, develop, and learn together and from one another as well as independently.
6. Be aware of the many facets of creativity besides arts and crafts: verbal responses, written responses both in prose and poetic style, fiction and nonfiction form. Creativity enters all curricular areas and disciplines.
7. Encourage divergent learning activities. Be a resource provider and director.
8. Listen and laugh with students. A warm supportive atmosphere provides freedom and security in exploratory thinking.
9. Allow students to have choices and be a part of the decision-making process. Let them have a part in the control of their education and learning experiences.
10. Let everyone get involved, and demonstrate the value of involvement by supporting student ideas and solutions to problems and projects.

Inquiry, Discovery, Problem Solving and Creativity

Problem solving is the process of recognizing an obstacle, difficulty, or inability to act; thinking of possible solutions; and testing or evaluating the solutions. The inquiry, or discovery, approach to learning has been labeled the complete problem-solving process. This approach has the unique advantage of making a learning experience meaningful to the individual learner.

The process of inquiry begins when individuals question something in their experience. The teacher can structure students' learning experiences in such a way that they will question. Once they begin to inquire, intrinsic interest takes hold and a learning by discovery process takes place.

There are three phases involved in the inquiry problem-solving process. The first is awareness, sensing that a problem exists. This is the motivating factor which arouses the student to go further in defining and resolving a problem. Once the problem is brought into awareness, the problem formulating stage begins. During this phase the problem is defined and ideas arise for plausible solution strategies. It is during this phase that information about the problem is gathered, usually through inquiry behavior such as questions and trial-and-error behavior. The next stage is searching. During this period questioning and information gathering begin to be associated with the formulation of viable hypotheses. Backtracking to reconsider and recapitulate on information may occur in this phase.

When all necessary information has been gathered and a plausible hypothesis had been formulated and tested, the problem solvers may feel their problem has been resolved. The answers to inquiry procedures may not always be a product of the same inferences and generalizations, even within the same manipulative situation, for the inquiry process is individualized according to any one individual's questioning pursuits and interests. The inquiry approach is necessarily a divergent thinking technique. Each student will approach the problem with a unique background of experience and focus and direct activities towards goals that are real and meaningful.

Inquiry techniques work well in the classroom in which a warm, open classroom atmosphere prevails. Conditions that foster creativity will also promote inquiry, for students involved in a discovery process must feel free to combine new ideas, ask questions, share their thoughts and reactions, and express their ideas without excessive pressure of peer competition.

Inquiry-discovery teaching is an indirect teaching method. The teacher becomes a guide and facilitator to set students on the road to discovery. The teacher must supply information and materials as students need and inquire about task relevant information. Inquiry learning involves manipulation of the learning environment which is meaningful and relevant to students. A variety of well selected materials can serve to guide students towards the discovery of concepts and principles. Environments in which students are free to choose alternative instructional materials tend to increase inquiry activity.

The use of media is especially appropriate to the introduction of problems and the exploration of ideas and hypotheses which students formulate. Learning centers, for example, provide the necessary freedom of manipulation and availability of materials which inquiry learning requires. Small groups are an excellent means of hypothesis testing and physical manipulation of materials, and role playing is a natural outlet for testing and manipulating social problems and questions.

In all situations, students are actively and meaningfully involved in a personal learning situation. Children will sense problems, ask questions, request and gather information before making decisions when decisions are necessary but no specific problems demand solution. "Inquiry, in essence, is the pursuit of meaning by seeing if one's own ideas about an object, or phenomenon, are substantiated by one's actual experiences with, or observations of it (Strain, 1970, p. 117)."

Creativity is inherently related to the discovery process. Creativity is present in the production of questions and hypotheses, and in the combination of known facts and principles into manipulations of the unknown and development of solution strategies. Experience with discovery learning enhances creative performance by forcing the learner to manipulate the environment and produce new ideas.

The learner must be flexible to examine alternative solution strategies and hypotheses, and must elaborate and define needs in the quest for information. All of the creative processes, fluency, flexibility, elaboration, and originality are thus incorporated in the discovery-inquiry problem-solving process.

The basic considerations to be met in an inquiry learning experience are:

1. Provide the initial experience to interest students in inquiring about a problem, concept, situation, or idea. The use of media, role-playing, and demonstrations are generally successful investigative starters. Learning centers with a number of viable options are an excellent beginning.
2. Provide the students with manipulative situations and materials to begin avenues of exploration. Games, media, files, sourcebooks, and discussions are all good starters.
3. Supply information sources for students' questions. Outside sources, field trips, speakers, peers, and the teacher are good supplements to written sources. The community and the world at large are fair game in the information seeking stage.
4. Provide materials and equipment that will spark and encourage student experimentation and production.

34

5. Provide time for students to manipulate, discuss, experiment, fail, and succeed.
6. Provide guidance, reassurance, and reinforcement for student ideas and hypotheses.
7. Reward and encourage acceptable solutions and solution strategies. Use failing experiences as instructional motivators. Have children question why a solution will not work and ask open-ended questions. A supportive positive climate will spawn the best results.

Expecting the Unexpected:
Questioning Techniques

In order to help children become good thinkers, we need to give them something to think about. The most common method of getting children to think is to ask questions. However, asking questions that require children to think requires much more thought and preparation by the teacher than asking questions which have one correct response. Convergent questions that have one right answer are useful in evaluating the learning of information, but they require few thinking skills on either the part of the teacher or the learner.

Questions which facilitate creative thinking are divergent or open-ended questions. These questions are often the springboard for a discussion because they have a number of possible answers.

Open-ended questions are stimulating if the children express interest in the subject area, and they may evoke questions from the students as a consequence of the teacher's questioning. In order to be effective, open-ended questions must deal with material familiar to the students.

Divergent questions can provide access to all of the cognitive skills children need to acquire. Questions can be asked at all thinking levels and abilities. Higher level questions (analysis and evaluation) produce better evaluative skills than do the questions on lower levels. Questioning divergently helps children develop skills in gathering facts, formulating hypotheses, and testing their information.

Questioning also supplies valuable information to the teacher. Carin lists seven reasons teachers ask questions in his article "Techniques for Developing Discovery Questioning Skills":

1. To arouse interest and motivate children to participate actively in a lesson.
2. To evaluate pupils' preparation and to see if their homework or previous work has been mastered.
3. To review and summarize what is taught.
4. To develop insights by helping children see new relationships.

5. To stimulate critical thinking and development of questioning attitudes.
6. To stimulate pupils to seek out additional knowledge on their own.
7. To evaluate the achievement of goals and objectives of lessons. (Carin, 1970, p. 14.)

Here are some guidelines to follow in developing your own questioning techniques:

1. Prepare questions before a lesson.
2. Ask questions simply and directly and avoid excessive wording. Vary the way you word questions. Ask Questions which stimulate students' creative thinking processes (comparison, just suppose, interpretation, criticism, etc.).
3. Use some simple information questions to break the ice and to induce student participation, particularly for children who are fearful about responding to thought questions.
4. Allow sufficient time, after a question is asked, for children to think and to formulate possible answers or responses. Avoid calling on the first student whose hand is up.
5. Reinforce and encourage all children's efforts to respond even though their contributions might be wrong. If a child's response is incorrect, offer a correction or call for a response from another child, but try to avoid any sense of ridicule or "put down" of the child whose response was wrong.

Here are some illustrative questions based on the concepts of fluency, flexibility, and originality for a lesson on the Pony Express:

Fluency: What are all the ways mail might have been transported across the United States at that time?

Flexibility: Most of the time we think of the horse as a means of transportation for the rider and mail. Can you think of other ways a horse could have been used to communicate information from one place to another?

Originality: Can you think of some very unusual way that no one else has thought of to transport mail today?

Questions to induce higher level thinking can also be developed using Guilford's Structure of Intellect operations as a guide (Guilford, 1971). The operations are memory, cognition, divergent thinking, convergent thinking, and evaluation. Examples of questions at each level of operation are presented next.

Memory: Where did the battle take place?

Cognition: What did Sam mean when he said "They'll rue this day."

Divergent: What if the battle had never started? What would have been the course of events in Russia?

Convergent: How did social and economic factors combine to alter the course of the war?

Evaluation: In your opinion was the Vietnam war justified?

Memory questions call for simple recall of information. Cognition questions may call for comprehension or interpretation. Divergent questions call for creative speculation or for new ideas. Convergent questions pose a problem and ask for a solution. Evaluation questions ask for opinions, judgment or decisions based on values.

Questions to induce higher level thinking can also be based on the Bloom Taxonomy (1956). The six levels of the taxonomy are (1) knowledge, (2) comprehension, (3) application, (4) analysis, (5) synthesis, and (6) judgment. Examples of questions at each level follow:

Knowledge: List the major causes of World War I as stated in Jones' text.

Comprehension: Explain the concept of detente and give illustration of detente in action.

Application: If the temperature rises and the amount of gas pressure increases, what would be the stress impact on the metal container?

Analysis: What are the major components of a book? Compare and contrast their importance to the reader.

Synthesis: Using the concepts of gerontology, describe an ideal pattern of behavior in old age.

Judgment: Using standards of literary criticism, critique Jone's essay on modern education.

Some of the examples are suggestions for discussion, not questions. However, all reflect techniques for interaction between teacher and students. The higher level questions in the Guilford model are divergent, convergent and evaluation. In the Bloom model they are application, analysis, synthesis, and judgment.

With careful planning and practice teachers can develop higher level thinking skills with these higher level questions. Some questions at the lower levels will also be appropriate as a part of the total class discussion.

Critical Thinking

There is more to thinking than meets the ear. The ability to give the right answer to a question may or may not be a significant accomplishment, depending on the thought processes that took place before the answer surfaced. Critical thinking involves evaluation and consideration of the information available to the thinker. Critical thinking involves creative thinking because it requires the thinker to assimilate information and hypothesize solutions to problems.

Five basic steps are employed in the critical thinking process:

1. Recognizing problems.
2. Formulating hypotheses.
3. Gathering pertinent facts or data.
4. Testing and evaluation.
5. Drawing conclusions.

Classroom activities can be geared to developing critical thinking in students. Instruction must be organized in such a way that students are supplied background information and allowed to manipulate the information and discuss problems in order to discover their own conclusions. By learning to think critically, students learn to utilize and incorporate their acquired knowledge in a cumulative and productive manner.

Questioning and discussion sessions which employ divergent questioning techniques facilitate critical thinking. Students who are critical thinkers also need to be questioning learners. Situational learning which provides information but causes a student to seek information rather than to simply process given information will aid in the development of critical thinking. Learning by doing, role playing, solving cases and problems, and experimentation are situational learning experiences. Simulations are also excellent ways to actively involve students in a learning situation and to induce and teach critical thinking.

Critical thinking is the productive thinking ability that enables us to solve problems, plan and implement ideas and activities, and handle life without a floor plan or set of directions. It should be the most important phenomenon of learning for a teacher to develop, and it definitely is a creative, productive activity.

Ennis (1962, p. 84) offered 12 criteria of critical thinking:

1. Grasping the meaning of a statement.
2. Judging whether there is ambiguity in a line of reasoning.
3. Judging whether certain statements contradict each other.
4. Judging whether a conclusion follows necessarily.
5. Judging whether a statement is specific enough.
6. Judging whether a statement is actually the application of a certain principle.
7. Judging whether an observation statement is reliable.
8. Judging whether an inductive conclusion is warranted.
9. Judging whether the problem has been identified.
10. Judging whether something is an assumption.

11. Judging whether a definition is adequate.
12. Judging whether a statement made by an alleged authority is acceptable.

These criteria could be used as valuable guidelines to the teacher who is developing critical thinking activities in the classroom.

Brainstorming

Brainstorming is a technique used to produce ideas related to a particular problem, topic, or theme. It is an excellent technique for strengthening imagination, flexibility, and discussion techniques. It is also a highly successful tool for problem solving that can be conveniently used in nearly every subject area and situation.

All ideas should be recorded. If the "recorders" are writing ideas, two work better than one since the ideas sometimes come fast and heavy. A tape recorder is a good backup device to make sure no ideas are missed. It is also good to put all ideas on the blackboard because then they are available for all to see.

It is good to gather all participants into a circle if possible, but normal classroom seating in rows will also be suitable. Announce the topic well before the actual brainstorming session to allow students to think about the topic a while before the brainstorming session. When the session begins the topic should be restated and students should be told the ground rules:

1. Do not criticize or evaluate any ideas produced. Ideas should be free-flowing and unhampered at this stage.
2. Crazy or humorous ideas are acceptable. Wild, imaginative ideas may become practical when forced into problem situations from a different viewpoint. The emergence of an unusual or bizarre idea may spark yet another idea.
3. Quantity of ideas is important. Quality of ideas is not considered at this point. The more ideas there are, the greater the base for evaluating and selecting viable ideas becomes.
4. Work with others in the combination of ideas. No one person's idea belongs to that person; all ideas at this stage are thrown into the communal pot. Ideas that sprout from other ideas that have been suggested are fair game.

Participants should be allowed to express their ideas as they come, but one at a time so that all ideas are recorded. "Hitchhiking" is welcomed. That is, if one participant gets an idea from another's idea, he/she should be allowed to give the new response immediately. Combining two or more responses is acceptable and encouraged.

The secret to brainstorming is deferred judgment. This means that criticism is ruled out. All responses are accepted and evaluation (good or bad) is withheld until later. Some teachers like to keep a bell or buzzer handy to use as a warning signal that someone is criticizing or evaluating. Freewheeling is also welcomed. Wild, bizarre ideas are welcomed.

In brainstorming, the emphasis should be on quantity. Quality implies evaluation, which comes after the brainstorming session. Quantity is important. The larger the number of ideas produced, the more likely that many of them will be useful ones. The ideas generated tend to get more original as the session continues. Common ideas will be generated at first, then participants begin to stretch their minds for unusual responses as the less obvious responses are offered.

After the session is over, members should be provided with a typed copy listing all the ideas generated. This can be used for further exploration, combination of ideas, and final selection of potentially useful ideas. Evaluation and selection of ideas to be implemented or developed should come from each member or from a select committee *after* the brainstorming session. It is often a good idea to have a postsession request for late ideas and thoughts. Then students can be assigned to project work groups to plan, elaborate, develop, and implement the ideas.

The topic for brainstorming should cover the problem statement but be broad enough to allow for freedom of thought. For example, when brainstorming for a unit on the family in social studies class the question might be, "What are all the ways families could increase cohesiveness and togetherness?" For a unit on Japan, the question might be, "What are all the things we would like to learn about Japan?" In both instances, the ideas generated would be used as the foundations for developing other learning activities.

Brainstorming can be used in almost any area of the curriculum. Students can also be given problems in classroom planning and management (how to solve a trying discipline problem, things to be done in planning for a forthcoming field trip). In all instances brainstorming sessions should be followed by an evaluation session in which the best or most promising ideas are identified and plans are made for individuals or small groups to work on developing, elaborating, and implementing them.

Attribute Listing

The combination or modification of old ideas, concepts, and principles into new and novel ones is the basic premise behind creative thinking. Attribute listing is a technique that promotes a clearer view of the qualities, specifications, characteristics, limitations, and attributes of a problem to allow for easy change and the development of new ideas through the change.

Part or Component	Characteristics or Attribute	Ideas for Improvement
1. The ground surface	1. Grass Blacktop Concrete	1. Need more grass Use artificial turf
2. The placement of play equipment	2. In rows Close together	2. Vary placement Spread out Make game area
3. The baseball diamond	3. At far corner On dirt area	3. Put in grass Stationary bases
4. The swings	4. Very tall Metal chain Wooden seats	4. Need small ones Belt seats better
5. The water fountains	5. One fountain Made of concrete	5. Need more fountains Needs steps
6. The fence around it	6. Very high Chain link Blocks vision	6. Make it lower More open

Figure 4.1. Problem: How to improve the playground

Paper and pencil, chalkboard, transparency material, and an overhead projector are the main items of equipment needed. Attribute listing can be done by individual children or combined with informal brainstorming in group work.

The teacher can begin an attribute listing group project by defining the problem and writing it where it is readily visible to all the children. Then a chart such as appears in Figure 4.1 should be developed. In column form, three lists should be developed. In the first column, the problem is broken down into parts or components. In column two, the characteristics or attributes of each part are listed. In column three, ideas for improvement, based on ideas generated in columns one and two, are written.

After the ideas have been developed and listed they can be easily examined, discussed, and elaborated upon. If they pass the evaluator and receive approval from the group, the final step is implementation and resulting modification or solution of the problem.

Attribute listing can be used as a springboard for stimulating class discussions. The possibilities are endless. Social studies discussions, discussions of scientific principles and problems, character studies and story writing and discussions, and problem solving are some suggested areas in which attribute listing can be used.

Attribute listing could take place in large class discussions, in small group work, or individually. One idea is to supply handouts with column one already filled in. Attribute listing is a useful technique for developing new ideas.

Morphological Analysis

The technique of *morphological analysis* involves studying two or more components of a problem. Whereas attribute listing or "check-list" techniques focus on modification principles, morphological analysis focuses on a principle of *combinations*. In morphological analysis, then, we try to combine existing data or parts of a problem in new ways, to discover original ideas or solutions.

Morphological analysis usually employs a grid or matrix to help us study as many combinations as possible, in a systematic manner.

Parameters. We begin by identifying the basic dimensions or components of the problem, which are called *parameters*. Although any problem might be analyzed using a large number of parameters, it is usually easiest if you try to identify from *two* to *four or five* basic components. For illustrations, problems can most easily be represented by two or three parameters (which can be drawn as a square or a cube).

For example, in Figure 4.2, we have considered the problem, "How might we improve the classroom environment using common materials and available equipment?" In this example, there are two parameters: *components of the classroom,* and *available materials.*

A second example involves the problem, "What are some effective ways of creating program options for gifted students?" This problem, illustrated in Figure 4.3, has been analyzed using four parameters: *people* who might work with gifted students, *places* where learning might occur in unique ways, *processes to be encouraged, and products* which might result.

Attributes. After listing the parameters of the problem, the next step is to list the *attributes* for each parameter. For example, the components of the classroom in Figure 4.2 (which are attributes) were: floors, walls, desks, tables, and chalkboards. The attributes of the other parameter, materials, were: paper, cardboard, felt-cloth, etc.

Once the attributes are listed, the next step is to *test all the possible combinations.* Try to find ways to combine each attribute of the first parameter with each of the attributes of the other parameters, to try to identify new combinations or original ideas. Not *every* combination will be productive, of course (in Figure 4.3, there are 50,625 possible combinations). However, it is quite likely that you will discover some new, unusual, and valuable ideas.

Materials	Components				
Materials	Floors	Walls	Desks	Tables	Chalk-boards
Paper	Paper footprints to guide movement	Murals for walls	Paper desk pads for scratch paper work		
Cardboard	Use large pieces of cardboard as room dividers	Partitions study carrells	Use Tri-wall cardboard to build desks	Put cardboard boxes on tables for storage	Could get more black boards painting black on cardboard
Felt/Cloth	Bring in scraps to sew together to make a classroom carpet	Put up felt/burlap strips for display purposes	Make cushions for desk chairs		
Paint		May not be possible to do in some schools	Let each child decorate desk	Have color-coded tables for learning stations	Slate paint on walls, ceiling boards
Rubber	Old tires for sitting in				
Glass		Partitions to cut sound and noise down		Glass tops to lay over desks and tables with instructions underneath	
Plastic		Egg carton wall partitions good acoustic devices			

Figure 4 ? Problem: Improving the classroom environment using common materials and available equipment

PEOPLE	PLACES	PROCESSES	PRODUCTS
Gifted Students	School	Basic Facts/ Information	Written Prose
Parents	Homes	Divergent Thinking	Solution — Action Plan
Teachers	Camps	Exploratory Experiences	Poems
Principals	Retreat/ Conference Ctr.	Problem Solving Steps	Songs/Music
Business People	Stores/Malls	Critical Thinking/Eval.	Visual/Artistic Media
Younger Children	Community Centers	"Higher Levels" (Applic/Anal/ Synthesis)	Story in News-papers
Older Children	Service Clubs	Research/Inquiry Methods	TV or Radio Program
School Board Members	Van or Mobile Center	Values Clarification	Movie, Slide, or Photo Story
Politician	Hotels/Motels	Independent Investigations	Dramatic Presentations
Civic Leaders	Parks, Zoo	Risk-Taking	Legislation
Retired/Sr. Citizens	Farms	Intuition	Construction/ Demolition
Counselor/ School Psyc.	Office Bldgs.	Complexity/ Challenge	Changing Commun. Attitudes
College Students	Corridors/Display Cases/Walls	Self-concept	Inventions/ Patents/Copyright
Scientists	Bus	Predicting Estimating	Videotape/audio
Professionals	Laboratories	Explaining	Monuments

Reprinted from G/C/T January-February, 1979, page 51.

Figure 4.3. Designing programs for the gifted and talented. Application of the morphological model.

44

Morphological analysis is a formal way of bringing ideas together into new possibilities and unusual combinations. It requires clear explanations from the teacher concerning what is expected from the students and how to accomplish it. Treffinger (1979) proposed six steps:

1. Selecting parameters
2. Listing attributes for each parameter
3. Developing evaluation criteria
4. Examining many combinations
5. Checking up on other resources
6. Following up on promising ideas

If problems are selected that are really interesting or important to the students, substantial motivation and interest will be generated. Morphological analysis, when carried out well, can lead to significant and useful solutions. Above all, the students learn a successful technique for thinking and solving problems.

Synectics

If I were an idea, how would I like to be formulated? Many people have played such imagination games. The name of the game is synectics, and it was developed by William J.J. Gordon (Gordon, 1961). Synectics is a creative thinking technique that utilizes analogies and metaphors to help the thinker analyze problems and form different viewpoints. No equipment is necessary, but it is a good idea to have paper or a chalkboard handy to record ideas. The first step is to define the problem and to state it on the chalkboard for all to see. Work then proceeds with the class as a whole led by the teacher or in small groups led by students.

There are three types of analogies popular for use in synectics: (1) fantasy, (2) direct, and (3) personal. The use of fantasy analogy is the most common and is usually the lead-off in a synectics session. In fantasy analogies children search for the ideal solutions to a problem, but their solutions can be as farfetched or unusual as possible. Solutions may be dreamed up in fanciful, whimsical, even animated dimensions. The teacher may start off a session by asking the children to think up the ideal solution for a problem involving movement of a heavy piece of equipment on the playground. Analogies may be fantasized that include tiny nymphlike creatures carrying the equipment skyward, use of elephants, or giant balloons. As in brainstorming all ideas are accepted, no ideas are criticized and children can build on one another's fantasies. After generating a number of fantasy ideas, the teacher leads the class back to a practical evaluation and analysis of the ideas to determine which ones might be practically developed.

Another popular form of analogy is the direct analogy. Using this technique, children are asked to find parallel problem situations in real life situations. The problem might be how to move some heavy furniture in the classroom. The problem might be paralled in real life situations by animals transporting their young. Spaceships carrying space exploration equipment would also be an example of the same problem situation in another setting. The main difference between fantasy and direct analogy procedures is that fantasy analogies can be entirely fictitious, whereas direct analogies must be actual parallels in real life to the problem. Again, all ideas are accepted, and the class tries later to examine the ideas for practical development.

Personal analogies require children to place themselves in the role of the problem itself. They might begin by saying "If I were a heavy swing set on the playground and I wanted to move to another place on the playground, what could I do? Well, I would reach up and pull down a big tree branch. Then I would release it and it would swing me to where I want to go."

The following narrative is illustrative of a synectics session. A fourth grade class is studying the organization of the post office. They have learned that breakage and damage is a major problem in the post office. The problem is written on the board as follows: How can heavy objects in the post office be moved with a minimum of manpower and maximum protection of the packages against damage? The class is taken on a field trip to the post office where they are told about the problems of package handling by postal workers.

After the return to the classroom, each student is asked to rewrite the problem on the board. Then the class identifies obvious solutions to the problem and writes them on the blackboard. Next, synectics discussion groups are organized. Each group must be led by the teacher or aides.

The leader begins with a fantasy analogy approach. Students are asked to imagine a situation in which packages are being moved. After a period of discussion, one student volunteers that the packages sprout arms and legs, and eyes and ears. The leader then asks for a forced combination of this analogy into the problem situation. The solution is then reexamined and it is suggested that the packages be placed on individual carrying devices that have remote sensing equipment and are self-propelled to a preprogrammed area.

Now, the leader asks for direct analogies. "What things move under their own direction and carry a heavy load?" Animals named are opossums and camels. A forced solution is then asked for between these animals and the problem at hand. Students hypothesize a device that is operated by pulleys and runs overhead, carrying packages suspended by hooks or magnets. This idea came from the analogy of opossums, which carry their babies clinging to their bellies. The idea of camels carrying weight between their humps is converted to mechanized carts with a large enclosed motor at each end, a carrying space between the motors, and a radar control system which directs the cart to a specified destination.

Finally, the leader asks for personal analogies. Students are assigned the role of packages and asked how they would like to be moved. The answers indicate concern for careful handling. One student shares a desire to float through the post office and settle gently at a destination. Another student asks to be moved with tender loving care. Forcing these ideas into the problem situation suggests that packages be allowed to float in a conveyor tank filled with foam packing pellets to appropriate stations in the post office.

At the end of the synectics sessions the leader gives the results and they are recorded on the board. In a follow up session the ideas are reviewed and evaluated, and the class finishes the activity by writing recommendations for package handling improvement to the Postmaster General.

Synectics is a fun way to involve students in imaginative discussions and come up with unusual and workable problem strategies. Any subject-related topic can be examined in small or large group discussions. Giving students an explanation of the method to be used and examples will help stimulate an effective synectics session. Through synectics students can learn valuable strategies for solving problems.

Forced Relationships

The technique of forcing relationships is a strengthening activity which helps develop the ability to see unusual uses for things and the combination of ideas from different viewpoints. The technique has four major approaches which will be summarized below. These are listing techniques, catalog techniques, focused relationships, and arbitrary forced relationships.

Listing Techniques

In this technique the problem statement is presented to the students. A list of unrelated objects is then presented, or generated by the teacher or children. This list has no relationship to the problem stated, and may in fact be produced before the introduction of the problem in order to lessen the tendency to choose related objects. The children must take each object on the list in turn and associate it with the problem statement. The objects themselves do not need to be related. The relationship should be derived by a free association method, that is, taking the first relationship that comes to mind. By doing this, judgment of the relationship is initially deferred. After all relationships have been recorded, the students go back through the list and evaluate the ideas for possible modification, development, and implementation.

Evaluation of the responses should be recorded with a + or −. A third run through the responses serves as a planning stage to begin development of the ideas.

Here is an example of a forced relationship technique used to deal with the problem "Fighting on the Playground."

	List	*Freely Associated Responses*
+	magazine	Take magazines to playground for diversion of fighters.
+	grass	If they must fight, grass is better than blacktop, so plant grass.
−	oil	Oil shoes of the fighters so they can't stand up.
−	shoe	Make the fighters go barefoot in warm weather. Blacktop and gravel will hurt feet and prevent fighting.
+	puzzles	Give children puzzles to solve to calm them down.
+	ice	Use ice cream to reward good behavior.
+	typewriter	Let children type to reward good behavior.

Catalog Techniques

This technique is much like the listing technique. The problem is stated first. However, objects to be used in association with problem solutions are drawn randomly from a catalog. The catalog is opened at random and the child can use any object as seen there in creating a solution. The objects are then forced to fit the problem statement. The same steps of evaluation, development, and implementation are then followed as in listing.

Focused Relationships

Focusing relationships follow the same line as the catalog or listing techniques. However, the relationship of the objects to the problem statement is not completely random or arbitrary. The objects which will be forced to the problem statement should be preselected and in some way be relevant to the problem. For example, in the problem "Fighting on the Playground," typewriter would not be selected as a forceable object, but grass and shoe might

48

be. Playground equipment, boxing gloves, rocks, and blacktop would be relevant to the problem. As with the other technique, the relationship of the objects to the problem is freely associated, one object at a time. Evaluation is held off until all of the relationships have been created. Then development and implementation of the ideas are undertaken.

Arbitrary Forced Relationships

Arbitrary forced relationships do not involve the use of a problem statement. All that is needed is a group of arbitrary words, objects, or ideas. Two objects are selected at random and forced together. Ideas that are produced using this technique can then be developed. One good method of presentation is to fill a fish bowl with objects written on folded slips of paper. The thinker must pull out two slips, read the names of the objects, and force them together to create a novel idea.

Classroom Strategies

These forced relationship techniques can be fun activities for the whole class, or very productive activities for individual students. They can be easily adapted for use in learning centers, and for seatwork activities between longer activities during the day. Here are some suggestions for using forced relationships techniques in classroom situations:

1. Provide catalogs for students to draw objects from and a list of problems from which students may pick those which they find interesting or stimulating.
2. Use a fishbowl or an idea box in a corner of the room or make a bulletin board with an idea box. Display students' ideas and forced relationships.
3. Provide words in lists for students to associate with a problem. Have a competition between two groups of students using the same lists and two different problems.
4. Let students brainstorm relevant ideas and objects for a particular problem, and then force relationships between their list and the problem.

These techniques can be used in almost any problems situation, whether it is subject matter related, or related to other classroom activities. They provide excellent experience in associative thinking and help children become better creative thinkers and problem solvers.

Creative Problem Solving

Several models of problem solving have been developed under the rubric of creative problem solving. Generally these models *do not* involve single answer or single solution problems. Rather they focus on problems for which many different solutions may be feasible. All these models also give the student some opportunity to participate in the problem identification and clarification process. Single solution problems always involve a problem defined by someone other than the student problem solver. Finally the creative problem solving model is generally used with realistic, practical problems whereas single solution problems frequently focus on puzzles or unreal and impractical problems.

Torrance and Myers (1970) presented one widely used model in their book *Creative Learning and Teaching* (p. 78). The model involves five steps or stages. Torrance and Myers urged that attention be paid to setting conditions prior to attempting to solve actual problems. Students' basic creative abilities and attitudes can be developed with many excellent training programs currently on the market. There should also be a period of "warm up" and an effort to establish a supportive climate in which there is freedom to express ideas openly and stimulation to pursue good ideas. The steps in the Torrance and Myers model are:

1. Sensing problems and challenges
2. Recognizing the real problem
3. Producing alternative solutions
4. Evaluating ideas
5. Preparing to put ideas into use

Students can work individually or in small groups with some pacing and guidance from the teacher. The third step can involve any of the other creative thinking strategies we have discussed in this book such as brainstorming, synectics, attribute listing or forced choices.

Parnes, Noller and Biondi (1977) presented a model of creative problem solving in their *Guide to Creative Action* derived from the work of Osborn (1963) and Parnes (1967). The stages in this model, referred to as "CPS," are:

1. Fact-Finding
2. Problem-Finding
3. Idea-Finding
4. Solution-Finding
5. Acceptance-Finding

Stage one teaches students how to look at the "messes" with which we all must deal every day, and to be sensitive to information and knowledge already at hand. Stage two is concerned with techniques for determining the essence of a problem and with wording problems in ways that facilitate productive thinking and solutions. Stage three introduces and utilizes many techniques for generating ideas. In stage four the ideas are used to project and synthesize solutions, and criteria are developed for evaluating alternatives and ideas. Finally, in stage five students learn how to implement the solutions by developing a plan for action. This creative problem solving model has been widely used and evaluated with older students and adults and found to be readily learned and used (Torrance, 1972; Reese, Parnes, Treffinger & Kaltsounis, 1976). Specific objectives for creative problem solving were described by Treffinger and Huber (1975). This comprehensive list is presented in Figure 4.4.

Noller (1977) developed a shortened and simplified explanation of the CPS model in her small book, *Scratching the Surface of Creative Problem Solving: A Bird's Eye-View of CPS*. She stressed that the term "finding" which is hyphenated in each step accents the hunting, searching for ideas which characterizes CPS. She also noted that problems usually begin with a mess because everything is ill defined and poorly understood. Steps one and two move the problems solver to a clearer conception of the problem as a prelude and guide to finding ideas and solutions. Parnes (1977) has also provided guidelines for using the CPS material with gifted students, and Noller, Treffinger, and Houseman (1979) have provided a short book which can be used to illustrate applications of CPS in gifted education.

The first author of this book has developed and used two models of creative problem solving which he has found to be highly effective in teaching students the processes of CPS. The first model, illustrated in Figure 4.5, borrows from the models described above but is unique in several respects. In stage one students work in small groups and identify their own problem but within a curricular framework specified by the teacher. In the illustration in Figure 4.5 the framework is the energy crisis, possibly a social studies problem. Brainstorming is used to identify problems, and the evaluation process is used to select out first three, then one, most critical problems.

Stage two is a clarification process. Students are urged to discuss the problem by giving illustrations of it, speculating about causes and so forth. Stage three is then a problem specifying process. Here the problem is written in as precise language as possible, and students are taught some appropriate forms for problem statements.

Stage four involves generating ideas using all the good creative thinking techniques such as synectics and attribute analysis. Then in stage five students synthesize their ideas into a single composite solution which utilizes as many of their stage four ideas as possible. They also test the fit of their solution to the problem statement.

Finally in stage six students learn how to plan for implementation of their solution. How will the solution be put to use? Who will do it? What sequence of events will be followed? etc.

1. **Be sensitive to problems**
   Given a "mess" the student should be able to describe many specific problems which could be appropriately attacked;
   Describe many elements of a situation;
   Employ a checklist to extend analysis of possible problems

2. **Be able to define problems**
   Given a perplexing situation, the student should be able to:
   —recognize the "hidden" or "real" problem which may underlie the stated question;
   —broaden the problem, or redefine it by asking "why";
   —redefine or clarify the problem by changing verbs;
   —identify several possible sub-problems

3. **Be able to break away from habit-bound thinking**
   Given a description of a common situation, the student should be able to:
   —describe habitual ways of responding;
   —evaluate the effectiveness of those responses;
   —develop several possible alternative ways of responding;
   —select promising alternatives;
   —develop and implement a plan for using new responses

4. **Be able to defer judgment**
   In viewing a perplexing situation, be able to:
   —produce many responses;
   —give responses without imposing evaluations;
   —refrain from evaluating others' responses.

5. **Be able to see new relationships**
   Given perplexing situations or stimuli, be able to:
   —identify similarities among objects or experiences;
   —identify differences among objects or experiences;
   —list ideas for relating or comparing objects/experiences

6. **Be able to evaluate the consequences of one's actions**
   Identify a variety of criteria for evaluation;
   Develop many possible criteria for any problem;
   Demonstrate deferred judgment with respect to criteria

Figure 4.4. Specific objectives for creative problem solving

Figure 4.4. *Continued.*

7. **Be able to plan for implementation of ideas**
   Given a problem and a proposed solution or set of solutions, the student should be able to:

   —identify specific sources of difficulty in implementation;
   —use checklists to recognize and anticipate obstacles;
   —specify a plan for facilitating acceptance

8. **Be able to observe carefully and discover facts**
   Given a perplexing situation or experience, be able to:

   —list many attributes of the situation;
   —describe factors influencing observation;
   —describe difficulties in "changing one's viewpoint"
   —describe techniques for breaking the limiting set of past experiences;
   —describe the features, characteristics, and functions of important parts of the situation.

9. **Be able to use effective techniques for discovering new ideas**
   Be able to:

   —describe and demonstrate the use of several techniques for facilitating idea production (part-changing, attribute listing, morphological analysis, synectics, etc.)
   —describe and demonstrate the use of Osborn's "Idea Spurring Questions" for stimulating new ideas.

10. **Be able to refine strange ideas into useful ones**
    Given a problem and a selection of apparently "silly" ideas, be able to:

    —describe ways the ideas might be made more useful;
    —demonstrate ways to define and use essential criteria in evaluating ideas;
    —describe problems associated with vague criteria;
    —demonstrate ways of rating ideas and using the results to plan a course of action;
    —describe and demonstrate the use of analogy in finding new ideas

11. **Be able to describe and use a systematic approach**
    Be able to define, illustrate, and implement in a problem each of the following stages in creative problem solving: fact finding, problem finding, idea finding, solution finding, and acceptance finding.

12. **Be able to describe the influences of interpersonal relationships on problem solving, and to illustrate problems associated with interpersonal relationships**
    —Become aware of one's own potential and limitations
    —Work actively to attain potential and overcome limitations
    —Be willing to master new ideas and apply them in real problems;
    —Be willing to share problems and ideas with others.

Processes	I. **Problem Generation**
	A. What are some problems our country faces as a result of the energy crisis?
Fluency	
Flexibility	
Originality	Brainstorm problem identification.
Deferred	
Judgment	
Evaluation	B. What are the most critical and general problems? Pick 3, then 1
	II. **Problem Clarification**
	A. What are illustrations of the problem?
Analysis	B. What are things that *cause* the problem?
Evaluation	C. What are further problems caused by the problem?
	D. What are attributes, characteristics or dimensions of the problem?
	III. **Problem Identification**
Synthesis	A. State the problem in light of stage II discussion as precisely as possible.
	IV. **Idea Finding**
	A. Brainstorm for solutions
Fluency	1. What could we do?
Flexibility	2. What could be changed?
Analysis	B. Forced association
Originality	C. Attribute analysis
Deferred	D. Synectics
Judgment	E. Solving parts of the problem
	V. **Synthesizing a Solution**
Synthesis	A. Pick out the best elements from stage IV.
Elaboration	B. Develop a Gestalt-closure
Evaluation	C. Does it fit to the problem statement?
	VI. **Implementation**
	A. Who will do what?
Synthesis	B. How will it be done?
Evaluation	C. What temporal sequence will be followed?
Originality	D. What precautions and obstacles must be watched for?
Flexibility	E. Locations?
	F. How to overcome obstacles?

Figure 4.5. Example of creative problem solving

1. Begin by having children brainstorm in small groups problems they have on the playground. Remind them of rules:

     (a) someone records all ideas
     (b) everyone must contribute
     (c) state ideas briefly
     (d) there is to be *no* criticism, discussion or evaluation
     (e) quantity is a goal
     (f) they can build on one another's ideas
     (g) funny ideas are acceptable

2. In phase two the group evaluates the list, discusses the problem, selects the three most serious or important, then the one most important.

3. In phase three the children brainstorm solutions to *the* problem. Follow same rules as above. Solutions can be full or partial ways of solving the problem.

4. In phase four they take ideas presented in phase three and create a synthesis for a solution. The solution might be eclectic, but it should hang together.

5. Develop a plan for implementing the solution. Who, where, when, how? Write the plan and turn it in.

Figure 4.6. Example of a simplified CPS model

With practice students can become fluent in using the model for a wide variety of problems in English, social studies, science and career education.

The second CPS model developed by Feldhusen, is called "A Simplified CPS Model" and is illustrated in Figure 4–6. It has been used extensively with elementary school children. It is very similar to the model discussed above, but it places less emphasis on precise problem clarification and identification. In this model there is also less emphasis on curriculum problems. Children get experience in identifying and solving problems which are a part of their daily lives.

These creative problem solving models provide excellent opportunities for students to engage actively in the thinking skills illustrated in the left margin of Figure 4.5. They also learn a valuable and comprehensive strategy for dealing with personal and curriculum problems. Evaluation by the first author of this book of a large number of students and teachers who have worked with these CPS models indicates that they provide experiences which are enjoyable and educationally valuable.

Torrance and others (Torrance, 1978, Torrance, Bruch and Torrance, 1976) have also utilized creative problem-solving processes and procedures in developing an extensive program in *future problem solving*. Students from many school districts throughout the United States have learned how to use creative problem-solving procedures to deal with many problems concerning the future. Students from both elementary and secondary schools have participated in "Future Problem Solving Bowl" programs, which have been conducted for several years in Athens, Georgia (at the University of Georgia) and in Lincoln, Nebraska (at the University of Nebraska).

Summary

These various methods and techniques for teaching creative thinking, problem solving, inquiry, and critical thinking can be incorporated into the regular classroom subject matter or they can be organized as separate experiences for gifted programs. If they are related to subject matter, they will enhance both subject matter learning and the acquisition of skills in creative thinking and problem solving. It is important to remember that in using any of these methods, the goal is not to solve problems as such. Rather it is to help students develop their abilities to solve many kinds of problems in and out of school.

SOME POPULAR INSTRUMENTS FOR ASSESSING VARIOUS ASPECTS OF CREATIVE ABILITY

Feldhusen, J.F. *Creativity Self Rating Scale.* Gifted Education Resource Institute, Purdue University, West Lafayette, Indiana 47906.

Feldhusen, J.F. and others. *Purdue Elementary Problem Solving Inventory.* Gifted Education Resource Institute, Purdue University, West Lafayette, Indiana 47906.

Guilford, J.P. and others. *Creativity Tests for Children.* Sheridan Psychological Services, P.O. Box 6101, Orange, California 92667.

Khatena, S., and Torrance, E.P. *Khatena-Torrance Creative Perception Inventory.* The Stoelting Company, 1350 S. Kostner Avenue, Chicago, Illinois 60623.

Meeker, M. *A Rating Scale for Identifying Creative Potential.* S01 Institute, 214 Main Street, El Segundo, California, 90245.

Renzulli, J.S. and others. *Scales for Rating Behavioral Characteristics of Superior Students.* Creative Learning Press, P.O. Box 320, Mansfield Center, Connecticut, 06250.

Rimm, S.B. *Group Inventory for Finding Creative Talent.* Educational Assessment Service, Route One, Watertown, Wisconsin, 53094.

Ross, J.D. and Ross, C.M. *Ross Tests of Higher Cognititive Processes.* Academic Therapy Publications, P.O. Box 899, 1539 Fourth Street, San Rafael, California, 94901.

Taylor, C.W. and others. *Alpha Biographical Inventory.* Institute for Behavioral Research on Creativity, University of Utah, Salt Lake City, Utah, 84100.

Torrance, E.P., Khatena, J. and Cunnington, B.F. *Thinking Creatively With Sounds and Words.* Personnel Press, Ginn and Company, Lexington, Massachusetts, 02173.

Torrance, E.P. *Torrance Tests of Creative Thinking.* Personnel Press, Ginn and Company, Lexington, Massachusetts, 02173.

REFERENCES

Bloom, B.S. . *Taxonomy of Educational Objectives, Cognitive Domain*. New York: David McKay, 1956.

Carin, A.A. Techniques for developing discovery questioning skills. *Science and Children*, 1970, 14, 13–15.

Ennis, R.H. *A Concept of Critical Thinking*. *Harvard Educational Review*. 1962, 32, 81–111.

Gordon, W.J.J. *Synectics*. New York: Harper & Row, 1961.

Guilford, J.P. *The Nature of Human Intelligence*. New York: McGraw-Hill, 1971.

Noller, R.B., Treffinger, D.J. and Houseman, E.D. *It's a gas to be gifted: CPS for the gifted and talented*. Buffalo: DOK, 1979.

Noller, R.B. *Scratching the Surface of Creative Problem Solving: A Bird's Eye View of CPS*. Buffalo: DOK Publishers, 1977.

Osborn, A. *Applied Imagination*. New York: Scribners, 1963.

Parnes, S.J. *Creative Behavior Guidebook*. New York: Scribners, 1967.

Parnes, S.J., Noller, R.B., and Biondi, A.M. *Guide to Creative Action*. New York: Charles Scribner's Sons, 1977.

Parnes, S.J. Guiding creative action. *Gifted Child Quarterly*, 1977. 21, 460–476.

Reese, H.W., Parnes, S.J., Treffinger, D.J., and Kaltsounis, G. Effects of a creative studies program on Structure of Intellect Factors. *Journal of Educational Psychology*, 1976, 68, 401–410.

Strain, L.B. Inquiry and social studies for disadvantaged learners. *The Social Studies*, 1970, 61 (4), 147–199.

Torrance, E.P. Can we teach children to think creatively? *Journal of Creative Behavior*, 1972, 6, 111–143.

Torrance, E.P. Helping your G/C/T child learn about the future. *G/C/T Magazine*, 1978, 1 (#1), 5+28−29.

Torrance, E.P., Bruch, C.B., and Torrance, J.P. Interscholastic futuristic problem-solving. *Journal of Creative Behavior*, 1976, 10, 117–125.

Torrance, E.P. ,and Myers, R. *Creative Learning and Teaching*. New York: Dodd, Mead, 1970.

Treffinger, D.J. 50,000 Ways to Create a gifted program. *G/C/T Magazine*, January-February 1979, pp. 18–19.

Treffinger, D.J., and Huber, J.R. Designing instruction in creative problem-solving. *Journal of Creative Behavior*, 1975, 9, 260–266.

ADDITIONAL REFERENCES ON METHODS FOR TEACHING CREATIVITY AND PROBLEM SOLVING

Davis, G.A. *Psychology of Problem Solving: Theory and Practice*. New York: Basic Books, 1973.

Stein, M.I. *Stimulating Creativity. Volume 1: Individual Procedures*. New York: Academic Press, 1974.

Stein, M.I. *Stimulating Creativity, Volume 2: Group Procedures*. New York: Academic Press, 1975.

Torrance, E.P., and Myers, R. *Creative Learning and Teaching*. New York: Dodd, Mead and Company. 1970.

Treffinger, D.J. Methods, techniques, and educational programs for stimulating creativity: 1975 Revision. In: Parnes, S.J.; Noller, R.B.; and Biondi, A.M. *Guide to Creative Action*. New York: Charles Scribner's Sons, 1977.

Chapter 5

HOW TO GET A PROJECT STARTED IN YOUR CLASSROOM

By now, you are probably ready to get started using some of these new ideas in your classroom. Even if you have already been doing some of these things (and we know that many good teachers are already using them!) we hope that you have found some interesting new techniques. The purpose of this chapter is to give you some practical suggestions about how to get started in an organized, exciting program to stimulate creative thinking and problem solving.

Six General Guidelines

Your efforts at helping children become better creative thinkers and problem solvers will be successful and more rewarding for you and your students if you approach your goal very systematically. There are six general guidelines which will help planning, conducting, and evaluating your classroom project. They are:

1. Know how to define creative thinking and problem-solving processes and abilities.
2. Be explicit in specifying the processes, skills, and content you will help the students in your class to learn and develop.
3. Try out your plans and new ideas before you begin to use them with your class.
4. Create an atmosphere in your class in which creative learning can occur.
5. Utilize learning procedures involving many activities and products.
6. Conduct a careful review and evaluation, not only of the students' learning, but of your own project and efforts, and plan revisions accordingly.

In this chapter, each of these guidelines will be discussed more specifically. We shall also point out some hazards and pitfalls you must be prepared to deal with during your project. We shall also offer some suggestions about opportunities for you to locate demonstration projects, and displays of useful resources and material are provided.

59

1. Know how to define creative-thinking and problem-solving processes and abilities.

At the very beginning, of course, *you* must be certain that you are clear and confident in your own understanding of creative thinking and problem solving. These are very complex processes of thinking and learning, and it is very important for you always to maintain a "sharp image" of your goals! We shall begin, then, with a brief review of some of the important ideas and concepts that you will want to keep in mind. First, we will review the nature of the problem-solving process, and then several more specific creative-thinking abilities.

What are the components of the problem-solving process? Many writers have taken up this question, of course, and their responses have usually been quite similar. Problem solving has often been described as a series of stages from finding and structuring a puzzling phenomenon to testing a solution and putting it to use. For our purposes, we will review the various components or "stages" using the method described by Parnes and his colleagues (Parnes, 1967; Parnes, Noller, and Biondi, 1977), called the *Creative Problem Solving* approach.

Parnes (1967) described a five-stage process: (1) fact finding, (2) problem finding, (3) idea finding, (4) solution finding, and (5) acceptance finding. Let's examine each of these stages.

Fact Finding involves using all of the information available about the problem. The problem solver must first examine all of the available information available. Before a problem can be solved, you must sift through all the data. You may not even be able to define the problem until you examine as much information as possible about "the mess" that puzzles you. You must become aware of any and every particle of information that might help to define the elusive problem.

Problem Finding. Once all information is collected and the clues to the problem are laid out, the task of *problem finding* or problem definition presents itself. In this stage, children are like a sponge. They absorb information about the components of the problem. When thoroughly saturated, they can evoke a broader restatement of the problem. By wringing information out of the sponge and soaking it back up several times, children can analyze each element in the problem, arrange and rearrange the problem statement, and define the objectives of the problem. Finally, the problem may be broken down into subproblems, and each component of the subproblems analyzed for available information.

Idea Finding. This is the generation and manipulation of ideas. Once the problem has been adequately defined, and all information about the problem and the problem situation has been identified, the task evolves into the generation of ideas and alternative solutions to the problem. Chapter 4 included several methods and strategies for producing ideas. Among these were brainstorming, checklisting, attribute listing, and morphological analysis.

Parnes (1967) and Osborn (1963) have emphasized that the principle of *deferred judgment* is extremely important during idea finding. At this stage, our focus should be on finding as many ideas as possible, and premature or excessive evaluation may inhibit valuable contributions. It is much easier to go back over our list of ideas later to evaluate them than to retrieve one lost spark of imagination. Remember the four "ground rules" for brainstorming which were discussed in the previous chapter; they are useful to employ during the idea-finding stage.

Solution finding. After a list of ideas has been formulated, the best and most practical or desirable idea to solve the problem must be sought. Herein lies the basis of the *Solution Finding* stage in problem solving. Solution finding is the evaluation of ideas produced in the idea-finding stage, and the manipulation of the best idea into a solution strategy. Now is the time for consideration and discussion of each idea that was produced. Criticism may indeed occur here, along with speculation and elaboration about possible ways to implement an idea. In the final analysis, the best idea may often turn out to be an unconventional idea, or one that may involve radical change.

Acceptance Finding. This is the final step in the creative problem-solving process. During this stage you undertake a final consideration of the solution in order to decide how best to implement it. Acceptance finding is concerned with helping good ideas become useful ideas.

What are some of the basic creative-thinking abilities with which you should also be concerned? There are several of these basic thinking abilities; each of them contributes to the creative problem-solving process, and can be encouraged in your daily instruction.

Creative-thinking abilities have also been the focus of the attention of many writers and program developers. Indeed, many of the instructional materials and programs that we have reviewed in this book emphasize the development of such abilities.

In defining creative-thinking abilities, it is common to emphasize four basic abilities that involve *divergent* thinking (Guilford, 1967; Torrance, 1962, 1966). These are fluency, flexibility, originality, and elaboration.

Fluency is thinking of many possible ideas or responses; it is a memory process. An individual gathers and stores information in his mind until it can be of use. Fluency can be observed in a class discussion when a pupil offers many ideas on one topic, or produces several ideas for the implementation of another individual's idea. Fluency is an important aspect of any idea generating component. A student who provides many responses in an idea producing session is illustrating fluency in thinking.

Flexibility is the ability to switch from one train of thought to another or to look at a problem in a new and different way. In problem solving and creativity, we must be able to look for a wide variety of applications or new kinds of ideas. Flexibility requires that we adapt to alternatives and find new situations and ideas. It also means not getting "locked into" rigid ways of viewing the problem. Flexible thinkers can use information in a variety of ways. Flexibility can be observed in a class discussion when a pupil switches easily from one topic to another and incorporates several alternatives to each problem presented. A student who gets stuck on one idea, or who cannot relate his/her ideas to other pupils' ideas, is not being flexible.

Originality is the ability to produce novel, unique, or unusual ideas. Unusual ideas are the combination of two old ideas in a new dimension. The invention to the water bed may have originated from someone's desire to float off to sleep. Originality can be strengthened in students, by practice, acceptance of unusual ideas, and encouragement for students to go out on a limb and "dream up" ideas.

Elaboration is the ability to fill out an idea, to add interesting details, and to build up groups of related ideas. Once an idea has been formulated, an individual must be able to bring it to fruition. Elaboration is also important in the fact-finding stage. Once you define an element of the problem, you must be able to clarify and elaborate on how it relates to the conditions of the problem.

2. Be explicit in specifying the processes, skills, and content you will help the students in your class to learn and develop.

In this recommendation we are concerned with developing goal statements and instructional objectives. Some teachers do not believe it is necessary or important to prepare specific instructional objectives. However, planning goals and objectives is an important step in preparing instruction which will effectively *foster* creative thinking and problem solving.

The development of objectives which contribute to your efforts to foster creative thinking takes into account the *content* (or subject matter) that will be taught. You should also deliberately consider the processes and abilities in creative thinking and problem solving, however, and check to insure that you have written objectives which involve the use of those processes and abilities. Some examples of statements of objectives which involve creative-thinking abilities and problem-solving processes have been provided by Covington, Crutchfield, Davis, and Olton (1972) in the Teacher's Guide for the *Productive Thinking Program*. Their summary of the skills of productive thinking includes:

> Recognizing puzzling facts
> Asking relevant, information-seeking questions
> Solving problems in new ways
> Generating ideas of high quality
> Evaluating ideas
> Achieving solutions to problems

The first author of the book has also worked with a school corporation in developing a set of cognitive objectives for a gifted program at the elementary level. They are presented in Figure 5.1. Note that these objectives relate to creativity and problem solving, independence and self direction in learning (10,11) and to language skills (12). In the same project the affective and social goals presented in Figure 5.2 were developed.

---

1. PRODUCE MULTIPLE IDEAS FOR VARIOUS COGNITIVE TASKS (FLUENCY).

2. THINK OF A WIDE RANGE OF IDEAS FOR DIFFERING TASKS (FLEX-IBILITY).

3. BE ORIGINAL AND CREATE RELATIVELY UNIQUE OR INNOVATIVE IDEAS (ORIGINALITY).

4. DEVELOP BASIC IDEAS AND FILL IN INTERESTING AND RELEVANT DETAILS (ELABORATION).

5. ASK QUESTIONS WHICH CLARIFY PUZZLING AND AMBIGUOUS SITUATIONS.

6. USE EFFECTIVE TECHNIQUES IN SOLVING CLOSED (SINGLE SOLU-TION) AND OPEN (MULTIPLE SOLUTIONS) PROBLEMS.

7. SYNTHESIZE IDEAS IN CREATIVE PROJECT ACTIVITIES.

8. EVALUATE ALTERNATIVE IDEAS OR SOLUTIONS IN PROBLEM SIT-UATIONS.

9. SENSE AND CLARIFY PROBLEMS IN A VARIETY OF SITUATIONS.

10. EXERCISE SELF MOTIVATION, DIRECTION, AND INDEPENDENCE IN LEARNING AND PROJECT ACTIVITIES.

11. CARRY OUT AN INDEPENDENT PROGRAM OF FREE READING AT A CHALLENGING LEVEL APPROPRIATE TO THE LEVEL OF READ-ING SKILL.

12. USE LANGUAGE EFFECTIVELY IN SPEAKING AND WRITING.

Figure 5.1. Cognitive objectives for a gifted education program at the elementary level

1. WORK WITH OTHER STUDENTS OF SIMILAR ABILITY IN PROJECT ACTIVITIES.

2. VIEW THEMSELVES AS COMPETENT AND EFFECTIVE LEARNERS.

3. RESPOND POSITIVELY TO VARIOUS TYPES OF COGNITIVE ACTIVITIES (FAVORABLE ATTITUDES TOWARD CREATIVE THINKING, PROBLEM SOLVING AND COGNITIVE PROJECT ACTIVITIES).

4. CLARIFY THEIR OWN VALUES SYSTEMS.

5. VIEW THEMSELVES AS COMPETENT CREATIVE THINKERS, PROBLEM SOLVERS, AND INDEPENDENT LEARNERS.

Figure 5.2. Affective and social goals for a gifted education program at the elementary level

In planning what will be taught, we also recommend that you can help encourage creative thinking and problem solving by involving students in making choices and in planning what will be learned. One way to do this is by planning several alternative learning activities, among which the students can choose, for each of your instructional objectives. If you wish to provide the students with an even greater role in planning, you can use class meetings at the beginning of a teaching unit or on a daily basis, at which time the students and the teacher can plan together. This approach can be supplemented very effectively by having another class meeting at the end of the day or unit, in which everyone reviews the progress that has been made and evaluates the extent to which the plans made earlier have been completed. Eventually, of course, the students can be brought into the planning process on an individual basis, through the use of contracts or learning agreements.

As you begin planning a project for developing creative thinking, you should also devote considerable energy to reviewing and selecting useful methods and materials. One source of guidance for task and method selection is Figure 5.3. This chart provides a description of several tasks which promote development in various aspects of problem solving. As you plan your project, a quick glance at the chart will point you in the direction of appropriate activities and tasks. You can use this information by looking to the methods and material available and choosing the materials that utilize the necessary types of activities for your purposes. The task chart is also a helpful tool when you are constructing or devising your own teaching materials.

Using Published Material

One early decision to make involves the extent to which you will utilize published materials, such as those reviewed in Chapter 6. The reviews in Chapter 6 provide enough information to help you make a tentative selection of suitable materials. If you locate some published material that seem to be appropriate for your project, you may be able to arrange to order it through your school's usual channels. (The information provided in the reviews may be helpful to your principal or supply coordinator in ordering the material.)

When the material arrives, scan the whole set to familiarize yourself with it. Then study the teacher's guide or manual quite carefully. The manual usually begins with a description of the purpose or objectives of material, and

Type of Task	Examples of Task Activities
Improvement	1. Product improvement—how could you make this product better.
	2. Situation improvement—how could you change this situation, environmental improvement, etc.
"What if" Situations	1. "Just Suppose" imagination activities. Story completion activities. Prediction of consequences.
Observation Activities	1. Finding camouflaged or hidden figures. Scrambled word games, word finding puzzles.
	2. Clue finding, information hunting in stories
	3. Problem definition. Defining a problem from a mass of information.
Questioning and Speculation	1. Speculating on what is occurring in a picture or part of a story.
	2. Writing newspaper headlines and story titles for pictures.
	3. Completing pictures and designs from abstract or symbol line beginnings.
	4. Solving riddles and puzzles.

Figure 5.3. Tasks useful in teaching problem awareness and information gathering: Sensitivity and awareness to problems. The discovery of problem situations and problem definition. Organizing available data, asking questions, classifying and utilizing information.

Type of Task	Examples of Task Activities
Ideational Fluency	1. Thinking up unusual uses for things, writing as much as possible about absurd topics.
	2. Writing similes, synonyms and antonyms for words and phrases.
	3. Categorizing—List all of the things you can think of that are cylindrical in shape.
Flexibility	1. Find a variety of uses for common objects.
	2. Make several drawings from line beginnings. Design symbols for words or ideas.
	3. Indicate subtle changes in phraseology, figural drawings, or visual demonstrations. (Find the figure that is different, where did the change occur, etc.)
	4. Find several solutions to physical puzzles (match stick puzzles, block puzzles, word puzzles.)
	5. Story problems—what endings might this story have, etc.
Improvement	1. Product improvement—how could you make this product better.
	2. Situation Improvement—how could you change this situation, environmental improvement, etc.
"What if Situations"	1. "Just Suppose" imagination activities. Story completion activities. Prediction of consequences.

Figure 5.3. Continued. Tasks useful in teaching idea production and formation of hypotheses: Thinking up ideas, finding ideas from available information and constructing hypotheses for problem solutions.

Type of Task	Examples of Task Activities
Elaboration	1. Adding details to drawings, designs, stories, or ideas. 2. Filling in outlines.
Associational Fluency	1. Writing synonyms and antonyms for words. 2. Producing lists of words that are associated with other words.
"What if" Situations	1. "Just suppose" imagination activities. Story completion activities. Prediction of consequences.
Experimentation	1. Manipulation of facts and actual trial of hypotheses through physical experimentation, simulated activities and games, role playing, etc.

Figure 5.3. Continued. Tasks useful in teaching evaluation and hypothesis testing: Making judgments about ideas and hypotheses previously formulated. Experimenting to test ideas. Generalizing consequences and results. Improving viable ideas, and checking hypotheses against the facts.

gives full instructions concerning how to use the kit. You should become thoroughly familiar with the various materials in the kit. Developers of materials often use special terminology when describing their materials. Thus it is imperative that you become familiar with each piece of material being described. This can be accomplished by handling and examining each piece of material as it is being discussed in the teacher's guide.

It is also important to read the complete description of how the material should be used. Some teachers who are highly competent in using traditional instructional material assume that they can bypass much of this material in the teacher's guide or manual. However, many innovative programs assume completely different teaching strategies emphasizing new methods of presentation, explanation, and student participation. Creativity and problem-solving instructional materials assume that there will be little presentation or explanation by the teacher and much stimulation of independent thinking. Because of the special nature of creativity materials, a thorough understanding of how to use the material to stimulate creative thinking and problem solving is necessary for maximum effectiveness.

The teacher's guide may also describe work that can be done to follow up the work in the kit being used or other sources that will enhance the kit. Clearly, the teacher's guide is a valuable source in which one may find, not only the way in which the kit can be used, but also ways in which auxiliary material or follow up work can be added in the classroom.

Using Methods

You may be interested in utilizing some of the methods for stimulating creative thinking, which were reviewed in Chapter 4. These methods can be useful in your project, whether you decide to make them the principal part of your efforts or whether you incorporate them into a program which also involves the use of published material.

After you have read Chapter 4 and identified some of the methods for possible incorporation in your project, you should plan to devote some additional time to preparation, since you will not have a teacher's manual or ready-made material for the pupils. It is important, of course, that *you* understand the use and limitations of the method. You may find it valuable to consult additional background references from Chapter 4 for any method you plan to try out, since each one involves specific techniques that must be quite clear to you before you will be able to use the method successfully.

When you feel confident that you understand the method, you should give yourself plenty of time to plan ways for "building" the method into your instructional plans.

Sometimes the method will be valuable to you in the *planning* stages of instruction. For example, brainstorming can be used with your class to plan the content of a unit or lesson (as was illustrated in Chapter 4). Alternatively, the methods may also be used in developing learning activities for the children, whether individually, in small groups, or with the entire class. Thus, you can use the methods described in Chapter 4 to plan instruction, as well as to provide a basis for learning activities to include in any lesson or unit plan you develop.

3. Try out your plans and new ideas before you begin to use them with your class.

It is likely that most teachers benefit from a trial run through the material as it would be used in the classroom before beginning their actual instruction. While it might seem laborious, this trial use of the material will yield substantial dividends. By doing this you will determine whether you really know how to use the material. Secondly, it allows for teacher anticipation. You have the prized and unmatched vantage point of knowing the needs, desires, problems, abilities, and interests of your students. With that information, plus thorough familiarity with the materials, you can be prepared for questions the students might raise and be able to direct them to follow-up activities. Great benefits can be realized if you are to direct your students to additional sources or activities when their interest or motivation is high. Furthermore, you can be prepared for the various problems that may arise while conducting the project in the classroom. These problems can range from the need for special equipment to inadequate time allocations for specific activities; they are easily eliminated by careful advance planning.

A trial run can be particularly useful if you are part of a "team-teaching" program, or if you can identify one or more of your colleagues with whom you can share your ideas and plans. If at least two teachers share an interest in a creative-thinking project, there will be many opportunities for the kind of sharing or "cross-fertilization" of ideas that is valuable in creative teaching and learning.

Finally, the trial run may be especially valuable if you are trying out a new method from Chapter 4, since it will provide you with an opportunity to verify your own personal understanding of the method and your ability to use it in your own thinking. You will be much more enthusiastic, probably, if you have had opportunities to put the method to use yourself before you begin to use it with your class.

4. Create an environment in your class in which creative learning can occur.

Creative learning does not just happen by chance, and while occasionally it might result from a "happy accident," one should not be satisfied with a project that depends upon luck. In addition, no amount of careful preplanning can reduce the importance of what happens in the classroom when the project actually begins. Every teacher has doubtlessly known the experience of the very carefully planned lesson that falls flat on its face. Fortunately, there are many things you can do to help prevent the fates from determining the success of your project in the classroom. Some of these things are described next under the general category of the "classroom atmosphere" you establish for creative learning.

Warm up

Before beginning a lesson or activity the teacher should attempt to "warm up" the class. Even the greatest lesson plan will not be effective unless it includes some strategy for establishing a receptive attitude among the students. One effective way of accomplishing this is by using open-ended questions which arouse interest or stimulate curiosity. Another effective approach is to utilize a puzzling phenomenon or problem to stimulate the students to ask their own questions. Many teachers give thought to *asking* different questions, but never think of the possibility of beginning instruction with spontaneous *student* questions. These "warm-up" methods are among those discussed by

Torrance and Myers (1970) in their very useful book, *Creative Learning and Teaching*.

Physical Arrangements

One important way of establishing a classroom atmosphere for creative learning is through careful attention to the physical arrangements of the classroom. For example, to use buzz groups effectively, it is necessary to seat small groups of students in circles. In some cases it might be helpful to push the desks aside and have the students sit on the floor. A brainstorming group can be as large as eight to ten students, while other kinds of group discussions, presentations, and demonstration projects may be best suited for an entire class.

If you are using an individualized approach in your project, you will probably also discover that you need to designate various parts of your classroom (or even other near-by rooms if they are available) for a number of individual and group activities throughout the day. If your room is large enough, you may well find it useful to use moveable dividers, portable chalk or bulletin boards, tables, or even home-made wooden or cardboard dividers to partition the room off into various activity areas. It is also worthwhile to include a special area for quiet relaxation and thinking; creative ideas often require a quiet period of time for "incubation."

Physical Activity and Productive Noise

You must also keep in mind that many creative-learning activities involve a greater degree of physical activity and discussion among students than are required by more traditional activities (particularly of the "seat work" variety). In your effort to develop a supportive environment for creative learning, don't work against your own purposes by being too rigid about movement, activity, and noise. There is an important difference, which you can soon learn to distinguish, between disruptive behavior and the "productive noise" and activity of children busily involved in tracking down new ideas and solutions to problems.

A stimulating classroom is filled with resources. There are things to explore, read, study and examine. There are many things on bulletin boards. There are places to relax and talk. The teacher encourages children to talk, to move about, to share ideas. The children do not drift aimlessly. There is no chaos. There is much active pursuit of learning activities. But the atmosphere is relaxed and pleasant. In such a room creativity and problem solving can flourish.

Deferred Judgment

In Chapter 4, in relation to brainstorming, you read about the principle of "deferred judgment." This is also an important principle for the teacher to remember in working to establish a creative learning environment.

Premature and hasty teacher evaluation can destroy a child's first efforts at creativity or problem solving. Creativity and problem solving are risky ventures. There are many blind alleys, false starts, failures, and frustrations. But children must learn to take the risks. This means that teachers must be slow to criticize. They should also help students to learn and practice the deferred judgment principle among themselves and avoid harsh criticism of each other's efforts. Children should also be encouraged to evaluate their own work, and given opportunities to learn how to do it, rather than being totally dependent on the teacher for evaluation.

Learning a Facilitative Role

When teachers first begin to consider the effects of increased student participation in planning, greater student independence in learning activities, and application of the principle of deferred judgment, it is easy for some misunderstandings to occur. Quite frequently, for example, an atmosphere for creative learning is confused with a totally "unstructured" or permissive atmosphere. It is best to avoid the term permissive, for it is extremely value laden and open to too many interpretations. Creative learning does place a great emphasis upon the active role of the learner in managing and directing learning activities independently. In many of the arrangements you develop to foster creativity, children will be somewhat noisier and more active physically than in traditional, self-contained, teacher-centered classrooms. But that does not mean that creative learning leads to children running around, screaming, shouting, or swinging from the light fixtures. Nor does it imply that *learning* is overlooked. In fact, it is true that children involved in creative activities will not only be working toward important goals and objectives, but will also be less likely to resort to aggressive and disruptive behavior.

Of course, the teacher must maintain some control over the class, but a low authority profile will have the most beneficial results. The teacher must act as a guide or facilitator when using creative methods. This means that the methods are student centered and not teacher centered. While relaxing control may be difficult, it is usually an essential ingredient in getting children to think for themselves. At first, the students may not be productive, but with encouragement, patience, and support they will make gains.

If the students believe they can realy on your constant support and encouragement they will be less hesitant to give a response that may not be a popular one. When students are able to give responses that are unpopular and infrequently given by other students, or even funny or ridiculous, they are more likely to think creatively. It is the teacher's responsibility to be accepting of the student's responses, to provide encouragement and reinforcement for all ideas, and to reduce or eliminate the criticism of the other class members. In fact it is better to allow the humor and fun to flow, since this usually accompanies creative ideas. You can help the class most by laughing along with them. This will serve to reinforce the students for their original and flexible thinking and show that you are really serious about encouraging creative thinking.

The teacher must be very open and receptive to the ideas of *all* students. The teacher should not show strong approval of some children's productions while showing disapproval of others that seem silly, funny, or unusual. Both quantity and quality of output will increase when evaluation is eliminated or at least postponed. This contributes to the supportive atmosphere that the teacher should try to foster, and reduces the fear and anxiety that inhibits creative thinking and problem solving in young children. The children must also learn to express appreciation or enjoyment of each others' work while avoiding criticism, ridicule, or sarcasm. The general classroom atmosphere should foster cooperative effort while allowing each child to think independently. The student must feel free to take risks in front of the other students and the teacher, and to express unusual, unique, or different ideas, without fear of ridicule. If students are embarassed or punished for what they say or do, it is not likely that they will make future attempts at thinking and presenting their ideas to classmates.

Finally, when you are attempting to establish a favorable atmosphere for creative thinking and problem solving, you must learn to develop a great deal of patience. You must be able to restrain yourself from "squelching" the child who is a constant source of new ideas. But, by the same token, you must also learn not to inhibit the efforts of students who are slower in getting started. They should also have encouragement, support, and adequate time for thinking about a problem.

In learning a facilitative role, then, it is suggested that you must (1) emphasize the student's self-directed learning as much as possible; (2) maintain a low authority profile; (3) accept ideas, whether common or unusual, from all students; (4) foster in your students and in your own behavior a sense of constructive criticism and an emphasis on self-evaluation processes; (5) strive to eliminate punishment or ridicule of new and unusual ideas; and (6) tolerate differences of time or speed among students in the ability to think up new ideas.

5. *Utilize learning procedures involving many activities and products.*

After your efforts in planning many and varied activities and procedures to help students engage in creative thinking and problem solving, and in developing a facilitative atmosphere, there comes the time when teaching actually starts. Now your challenge is to work with your pupils in ways that will promote the successful attainment of your goals. You will have to work quite regularly at maintaining the classroom environment and helping students employ many different abilities and skills in learning. While this may be a challenge, especially in working with children who have never encountered such efforts before, it is usually very exciting and satisfying for teachers and pupils alike.

There are some things you must be careful to remember, however. First of all, strive to find new and diverse ways for students to express themselves and demonstrate what they are learning. Too often it is easy to restrict ourselves to tests and written reports, although there are many other things pupils can do. You may plan specific alternatives, or allow the students to participate in designing them. Some other products to consider using in your class include: songs and music; murals, sculptures, or paintings; movement and physical expressions; community or school service projects; creation and production of original poetry and drama. You will find it valuable to encourage students to try their hand at expressing themselves in many different ways during a school year.

Creativity and problem-solving projects can easily be integrated into the daily classroom routine either as a part of a particular subject area or independently. Many teachers set aside some special time during each day for students to work on their projects as a class, in small groups, or as individuals. If a special time is set aside, you may find it easier to establish a creative atmosphere in the classroom during the period. However, creativity and problem-solving instructional materials can usually fit into any subject area that would normally be taught during the day. Many of the materials and methods described in Chapter 6 are specifically designed to be used as a part of the regular curriculum. Thus the *Purdue Creative Thinking Program* was designed to be used in social studies. Many of the materials are designed for use in language arts and some for use in mathematics and science. When used in this way the materials have dual benefits in that they not only aid in the development of some specific skill or knowledge but they also help to develop creativity or problem solving in students.

The use of small groups gives you and the students many advantages for creative-thinking and problem-solving activities. It reduces the fear and anxiety that may be associated with speaking in front of the whole class. Students are more likely to offer contributions when they are in a small, personal, closely seated group of people. Furthermore, the reduced number of students allows more time for each of the students to be presenting ideas, since each person in the group can talk more often than when the whole class is together. This may be especially helpful for students who speak infrequently or not at all. Small groups also allow students to proceed independently without supervision since the teacher can only visit with one group at a time. Small groups can also work at their own pace, going as slow or as fast as is appropriate for the group members.

You should also employ a variety of instructional techniques. Many teachers are already using large and small group discussion, some creative-thinking techniques (such as brainstorming), a wide variety of films and other media, and individualized instructional efforts such as learning centers or learning stations. These can all contribute effectively to creative thinking, problem solving, and inquiry by students. You may find it particularly useful, however, to use a contract or learning agreement approach to help students learn to use many instructional resources efficiently on their own.

6. Conduct a careful review and evaluation, not only of the students' learning, but of your own project and efforts, and plan revisions accordingly.

Your first concern in evaluation will probably be to seek effective ways of assessing the students' performance, and it is certainly necessary to do this. Creative learning does not imply that any concern for evaluation is dismissed. Although it is important to learn to *defer* judgment, there must come a time when you get down to the process of making decisions and assessing the quality of ideas and solutions. In relation to evaluation of the students, there are three specific suggestions you should consider. First, learn to define and use new sources of "evidence" in your evaluation. Do not feel constrained to evaluation using paper and pencil test scores and reports. By adopting a broad definition of evaluation, the questions you are striving to answer are: "Has the student reached the goal? How well has the job been done? What kinds of data do I have to support the decision?" Be alert, therefore, for *any* kinds of data to document the attainment of the goals and objectives by the students. Second, learn to use criterion-referenced evaluation, not just norm-referenced. It is not always necessary to compare students with each other. In creative-learning outcomes, it may frequently be much more appropriate to assess the *change* or *progress* made by the learner from one time to another, or to examine the success of the learner's efforts in relation to the specific goals that were defined. Third, the evaluation of creative learning and problem solving should increasingly be conducted *by the learner.*

You should also be concerned with evaluating your entire project. You may find it valuable to do this on a day-to-day basis and not just at the completion of the entire project. Again, you should begin by going back to the general goals of the project: why did you begin the project initially? What were you hoping to accomplish? Then, for each of your responses to these questions, ask yourself, "what kind of evidence would indicate whether or not that has actually happened?"

An important aspect of evaluation, which you should also remember, is that one purpose of evaluation is to provide you with a basis for systematic revisions of the program. Thus, after you have collected the evidence to evaluate your project, don't just use it to say, "It worked, or "It didn't work very well," and then drop it at that. Instead, seek to probe the strengths and weaknesses of the program, and try to look specifically at each factor thus identified. How can you improve the strengths? What can be done to revise the weaknesses? What new ideas should be incorporated?

Some Things to Watch out for

No matter how careful your planning and attention to the basic guidelines, things can go wrong. You cannot be protected from those problems and aggravations that can accompany any approach to instruction. But there are some things that you should be warned about, in the hope that forewarned will be forearmed.

First of all, don't give up when your first efforts are rough around the edges. Give yourself a fair chance to grow and to develop your own creative abilities. Too many times educational projects are dropped prematurely, with the first signs of difficulty, only later to have someone say, "Oh yes, I did try that once, and it wasn't any good." You must not be overcome with the frustration of a first attempt, but remember that with more experience, success will be easier to attain.

Second, creative thinking and problem solving, like any other educational concerns, can be handled in such a way as to become dull, boring routines. Your students will need variety, and there will be pressure upon you to create new ideas, and to keep on creating. Creative learning is not a venture for the teacher who wants to build a neat little package to use the same way, day in and day out. You will have to be prepared to work very hard to be flexible and original yourself.

Third, you will have to be flexible in responding to many more spontaneous, original ideas from your pupils. You won't have the cushion of the right answers in the teacher's guide to fall back upon. There will be times when you will have to say, "I don't know," and these occasions can be threatening to some people.

Fourth, you will have to deal with many more variations in time and daily schedules. Creative thinking and problem solving do take time. Individualized learning means that many children will be pursuing many different projects and activities throughout the day. At first, this may seem to be a state of chaos or disarray, but as you become more confident of the learner's efforts and your own organization, it will become much easier for you to tolerate.

Fifth, you must be prepared to create and maintain a constantly changing and growing pool of resources for learning. It won't do to put the goblins and witches up on the bulletin board in October and leave them there until the turkeys go up at the end of November. Nor will the reading table be adequately stocked with a few old books to last the year. There must be many different resources, and you will have to work hard to see that they are up-to-date and well suited to the changing interests and activities of the students.

Sixth, you may find that some of the traditional behaviors of teaching are difficult to change, particularly those which involve evaluation. When you look at someone's work, there may often be that persistent tendency to say, "Well, here's what you should do to correct this and that . . ." or "Let's see—this work is spelled wrong, and that idea isn't clear. . . ." It is difficult to learn to defer judgment, even when you know that eventually, evaluation will still occur. This will be a challenge to your own creative ability.

Seventh, it may be difficult at first to keep in mind that every child has the potential for creative thinking and problem solving. One must be concerned not only with a few children who display exceptional creative talent, but with providing opportunities for every child to develop these abilities and skills.

Eighth, some creative-thinking activities may be viewed by children as sex-typed. Creative dance, art, and poetry are viewed by some boys as girlish activities while mechanics, science, and sports are viewed by some girls as boy-type activities. Special efforts are needed by the teacher to overcome these sex-oriented responses. Above all, all creative and problem-solving activities should be experienced by both boys and girls. If the experience is rewarding, most of the problems will be overcome or at least alleviated.

Ninth, creativity and problem-solving methods and materials will demand a higher level of creative preparation from the teacher than traditional methods and materials. You will not be able simply to "follow the manual." More creative effort is needed to plan lessons, find materials, and guide ongoing learning activities.

Finally, you must make some decisions about your own values and commitments. You will be able to be most successful if you are concerned with fostering intellectual and personal growth in the individual child. You cannot view your job as mechanically "facing the little monsters every day" to get a paycheck if you are going to be successful in fostering creative learning, inquiry, and problem solving.

Summary

The ideas presented in this chapter imply careful, systematic planning of instruction. Some teachers will want still more specific guidance. Thus, we refer you to another publication titled *Reach Each You Teach* by Treffinger, Hohn and Feldhusen (1979). This book offers a comprehensive set of procedures, with illustrations, for developing instructional plans. It also focuses on how to plan for individualized instruction and on striving for higher level thinking processes in teaching.

REFERENCES

Covington, M.V.; Crutchfield, L; Davies, L; and Olton, R.M. *The Productive Thinking Program*. Columbus, Ohio: Charles E. Merrill Co., 1972.

Guilford, J.P. *The Nature of Human Intelligence*. New York: McGraw-Hill, 1967.

Osborn, A.F. *Applied Imagination*. New York: Scribners, 1963.

Parnes, S.J. *Creative Behavior Guidebook*. New York: Scribner's, 1967.

————. *Creative Behavior Workbook*. New York: Scribner's, 1967.

Parnes, S.J.; Noller, R.B.; and Biondi, A.M. *Guide to Creative Action*. New York: Scribner's, 1977.

Torrance, E.P. *Guiding Creative Talent*. Englewood Cliffs, N.J.: Prentice-Hall, . 1962.

————. *Torrance Tests of Creative Thinking*. Lexington, Mass.: Personnel Press, 1966.

Torrance, E.P., and Myers, R.E. *Creative Learning and Teaching*. New York: Dodd, Mead and Co., 1970.

Treffinger, D.J., Hohn, R.L., and Feldhusen, J.F. *Reach Each You Teach*. Buffalo: DOK Publishers, 1979.

Chapter 6

REVIEWS OF INSTRUCTIONAL MATERIAL AND BOOKS FOR TEACHING CREATIVITY AND PROBLEM SOLVING

This chapter presents the reviews of instructional materials and books on teaching creative thinking. The reviews of instructional material contain much specific information. Look at a sample review in that section. Then look at the headings described in Figure I. To the right of the headings are explanations of what each word or words mean.

The reviews will give you all the information you need to make a tentative decision as to the suitability of a kit or set of materials for your needs and interests. All of the reviews describe good, useful, productive instructional materials. Materials were included only after a careful inspection and review of a set indicated that it would be useful in teaching creative thinking or problem solving. When you settle on some materials which look interesting, you should read the entire review carefully.

The reviews of books on teaching creative thinking and problem solving are grouped together at the end of the chapter. These reviews attempt to show how each book would be useful to the classroom teacher.

Figure I

The Format of a Review of Instructional Material

What: This gives the title of the material and the author.

Published By: This is the name of the company publishing the material and their mailing address.

How To Order: This part gives three pieces of information. The first bit will tell you where to send your orders. Usually this will be the publisher unless otherwise indicated. If it is the publisher it will say "Order from publisher." Use the address given above in the "Published By" section. The second bit of information is the price of the material at the time it was reviewed. The final bit of information tells what item or parts of the material will be expended or lost as the kit is used in the classroom. These items can usually be replaced by the teacher or the publisher.

Description This section gives a brief description of the material, how it is used, and its most salient characteristics.

Target Audience: This section describes the grade level for which the material is intended.

Materials Provided: This section tells the quantity of the materials provided and names each piece that will come with the kit. The teacher should look at the "How to Order" section to see what materials will have to be replaced.

Teacher's Guide: If the kit contains a teacher's guide, this section will describe the guide and tell what you can expect from it. It will also tell about follow-up activities that are suggested by the guide.

Subject Matter and Teaching Strategy: This section describes how the material can be used in a variety of subject areas. You can use this information to plan how you will integrate a kit into your daily schedule, or use it to plan for creativity sessions in your classroom. The teaching strategy describes the suggested sequence of events that the teacher could use to teach a class. The use of the material with small groups, large groups and individuals is also discussed.

Rationale: Here the fundamental nature of the material is discussed. Its theoretical bases are described.

What:	*The Aesthetic Education Program* Cemrel Inc.
Published By:	Comenius Publishers Weston, Connecticut 06883
How To Order:	Order from publisher List Price: Varies, see catalog.
Description:	The Aesthetic Education Program is a unique system of materials, media games, and viewpoints which assist students in developing feeling and aesthetic responses. Such techniques as creating characterization; working with tone, shape, sound, movement; constructing dramatic plot; and creating word pictures help students develop their aesthetic abilities.
Target Audience:	Grades K–6.
Materials Provided:	The materials vary with each kit: Everything from student books and games to masks, magnetic tape and puzzles.

The available kits are:

Examining Point of View
Creating Word Pictures
Relating Sound and Movement
Tone Color
Creating Characterization
Constructing Dramatic Plot
Shape
Shapes and Patterns
Shape Relationships
Arranging Sounds with Magnetic Tape
Texture

Teacher's Guide:	The Teacher's Guide in this series includes notes regarding each concept in the student's books, objectives of the activities, and reduced reproductions of the pages of student books. Supplementary activities are also discussed. The Teacher's Guides are well illustrated and easy to use.

Subject
Matter
and
Teaching
Strategy:

The program involves the development of creative skills in reading, analogies, perception, identification of shapes, color, patterns, dramatic plots, sound, and movement.

The Aesthetic Education Program is effective in individualized and small group learning centers, as class projects, and as an integral part of a language or artistic skills program. Regardless of the way used, the *Aesthetic Education Program* serves as a valuable supplement to an educational program.

Rationale:

The *Aesthetic Education Program* provides guidance and experience in a wide variety of affective and aesthetic activities. The program uses the do and create approach. The activities require total involvement of the child including making decisions, developing ideas, and critical thinking. Through its rich and diverse activities children can learn to develop their affective, aesthetic and cognitive ability. In particular, the close relationship between cognitive creative abilities and affective dispositions should be developed.

What:	*Affective Direction—Planning and Teaching for Thinking and Feeling* Bob Eberle and Rosie Hall
Published By:	DOK Publishers, Inc. 71 Radcliffe Road Buffalo, New York 14214
How To Order:	Order from publisher List price: $7.50 Consumable items: None
Description:	*Affective Direction* is a working book for teachers, taking them progressively through the cognitive and affective processes in concise outline form. The book directs the reader through curriculum planning and classroom instruction, keeping in mind the authors aims—aesthetic sensitivity, interpersonal relations, moral-ethical development, and self-knowledge.
Target Audience:	Elementary and junior high school
Materials Provided:	One *Affective Direction* book
Teacher's Guide:	The entire book is intended to be used as a teacher's guide to the affective domain.
Subject Matter and Teaching Strategy:	The overall purpose of the book is to help educators teach for ethical and moral behavior. Several relevant goals are subsumed under the general purpose, including the aiding or understanding of the affective domain, the development of a general planning and teaching model, the classification and organization of instructional material from a design based on developmental theory, and the provision to teachers of a sense of direction in preparing instructional units. "Guideposts" and "checkpoints" provide the reader with a sense of direction and organization as he or she works through the book. A planning and teaching model is provided based on the cognitive and affective taxonomies. The model is based on the dimensions of content, processes, and strategies. *Affective Direction* may be used in several ways by the individual teacher interested in providing for student cognitive, affective, and personal growth, by teams of

teachers organizing instruction, by curriculum planners, by teachers of the gifted focusing on higher level thinking and feeling processes, and by teachers interested in developing creativity in students.

Rationale: The authors believe that an individual's self-concept, interpersonal relations, and aesthetic sensitivity largely determine his/her motivation and achievement levels. Development of the capacity to intellectualize has long been the domain of education. Educators are now being held accountable for solving many of society's ills, and affective goals have recently become a major responsibility of teachers. This book aids the teacher in understanding the need for affective education and in learning how to provide for it.

What:	*Affective Education Guidebook* by Bob Eberle and Rosie Emery Hall.
Published-By:	DOK Publishers, Inc. 71 Radcliffe Road Buffalo, New York 14214
How To Order:	Order from publisher. List price: $7.50.
Description:	The *Affective Education Guidebook* is a well-organized set of activities and instructional plans for teachers who are concerned with improving students' understanding and expression of feelings in the classroom setting. It contains more than 100 useful activities as well as suggestions for their effective utilization in the classroom.
Target Audience:	Elementary and Junior High School.
Materials Provided:	The *Affective Education Guidebook* presents a rationale for concern with affective education, an outline for a general plan (emphasizing program orientation, program planning, and program implementation), and more than 100 specific classroom activities. In addition, there are Appendices which emphasize group discussion skills, problem-solving guidelines, a plan for "building classroom community," and classroom techniques for relaxing and reflecting.
Teacher's Guide:	The *Affective Education Guidebook* is directed to the teacher, but it contains specific ideas and plans for classroom application too.
Subject Matter and Teaching Strategy:	The *Guidebook's* resources are intended to deal generally with the need to improve human relationships in the classroom. It should be considered resource material for "Affective Education." There are five levels represented in these resources: identification of many different feelings; steps toward the expression of feelings; provision for interaction and discussion of interpersonal relationships; new ways of exploring feelings; and authentic expressions of interpersonal regard.

Rationale: Drawing from the cognitive and affective taxonomies, and from the work of Frank Williams and others, the authors emphasize the ultimate goal of "a *community,* in which interpersonal bonds have been established, a higher level of human nature exists, and the sharing of psychic energy becomes possible" (p. 11).

What:	*Bewitching Tales* Joyce Kohfeldt
Published By:	Prentice-Hall Learning Systems, Inc. P.O. Box 47X Englewood Cliffs, New Jersey 07632
How To Order:	Order from publisher List price: $5.50 Consumable items: None
Description:	*Bewitching Tales* provides six units based on the theme "witches," stressing library skills, creative writing, art skills, dictionary skills, vocabulary development, and comprehension.
Target Audience:	Grades 4–7.
Materials Provided:	The 61 page book provides six units. Each unit contains tips for the teacher, samples of activity cards, and reproducible pages.
Teacher's Guide:	Each unit contains information for teacher preparation and "teacher tips" for using the material. A classroom wall chart is also provided.
Subject Matter and Teaching Strategy:	*Bewitching Tales* is designed for individualized utilization; strong emphasis is placed on language arts and related content areas.
Rationale:	The author describes the units as attempts to "integrate several different types of learning activities through a common theme—witches." The author stresses that the units provide opportunities for children to choose learning activities.

What:	*The Big Book of Independent Study* Sandra Kaplan, Sheila Madsen and Bette Gould
Published By:	Goodyear Publishing Co., 1640 5th Street Santa Monica, California 90401
How To Order:	Order from publisher List price: $15.95 Consumable items: Punch-out games and activity cards to be used in setting up independent study centers.
Description:	*The Big Book of Independent Study* is a collection of reproducible worksheets and punch-out games and activity cards printed on sturdy cardboard for use in introducing and reinforcing research skills and independent study. Subject areas include topic selection and definition, information collection and organization, and record keeping.
Target Audience:	Grades 3–6.
Materials Provided:	Besides the activities, games and worksheets ready for use in independent study centers, the *Big Book of Independent Study* also includes removable Teacher Information Cards with directions and suggestions for activities. The book contains tabs on each page to indicate activities and worksheets that go together as well as record keeping charts and skills list.
Subject Matter and Teaching Strategy:	*The Big Book of Independent Study* is designed to give practice in research skills, to provide a sequence of activities in conducting independent study, and to enrich the basic curriculum of a classroom. Suggested teacher adaptations include student-selected studies based on the students' own interests and needs, related studies in which students select topics after learning about a subject through the teacher's lessons, or curricular studies where the students select from a list of teacher-prepared topics based on subject matter studied by the class.

Teachers are urged to consider time, materials and space requirements in setting up independent study programs. Independent study may be used only with those students who are presently able to work independently, or the teacher may teach independent study skills to the entire class, replacing traditional lessons on a subject.

A section is included listing problems that may occur with the initiation of independent study techniques and possible solutions.

Rationale: By using carefully selected activities from this book, it is hoped several goals will be reached by the students: (1) learning how to learn; (2) actively seeking and gaining knowledge; (3) practicing decision making; (4) becoming self-sufficient learners; and (5) learning something of personal value.

What:	*Bright Ideas: Complete Enrichment Units from a Gifted Resource Room* Ellen Tan, Pam Piwnica, Sue Parker
Published By:	Creative Teaching Press 5305 Production Dr. Huntington Beach, California 92649
How To Order:	Order from publisher List price: $6.95 Consumable items:
Description:	This book provides a collection of lessons and activities for supplementary enrichment in the elementary classroom. Each chapter includes background information for the teacher, activities for students, and reproducible student activity pages.
Target Audience:	Grades 4–8.
Materials Provided:	The 107 page book is divided into eleven chapters: photography, publishing, poetry, tower of self, geometric line drawing, weaving, machines, the law, body fat, the heart at work, and blood pressure.
Teacher's Guide:	Each chapter provides specific directions for both teachers and students.
Subject Matter and Teaching Strategy:	The activities span a variety of subject areas, and include some activities which could be related to several content areas.
Rationale:	Although the activities are described as having been selected for their interest to gifted students, they actually seem to be activities that would be appealing and valuable to many students. They stress topics of considerable interest to students, and emphasize active participation. They provide examples of what Renzulli's Enrichment Triad Model would classify as "Type I" enrichment materials.

What:	*Brown Paper School Books* Developed by Yolla Bolly Press Covelo, California
Published By:	Little, Brown and Company 34 Beacon Street Boston, Massachusetts
How To Order:	Order from publisher List price: $4.95/book Consumable items: None
Description:	The *Brown Paper School Books* is an appealing series of humorous and imaginative books, each containing entertaining activities designed to teach the child concepts and at the same time keep intact the student's joy and enthusiasm for learning.
Target Audience:	Grades 5–8.
Materials Provided:	Each book may be purchased separately and is an entity in itself. Several of the selections are listed here:

The I Hate Mathematics Book—A book that teaches children that mathematics is simply a way of looking at the world, a tool to be used in situations of every child's life. Includes mathematical events, gags, magic tricks and experiments.

My Backyard History Book—A local history book based on the concept that learning about the past best starts at home. History includes more than memorization and facts about people long dead; it studies the passing of time. Projects deal with making time capsules and tracing genealogy among other activities.

The Book of Think—This book teaches problem solving techniques in a variety of situations. Children learn to recognize a problem when they encounter one, to sharpen their senses and to stretch their brains. They gain practice in seeing more than one correct answer and tackling problems in different ways.

I Am Not a Short Adult—Deals with the affective aspects of being a child, including family, school, money, ethics, adulthood, work and play, and making the most of childhood.

The Night Sky Book—An astronomy book for children that teaches them about constellations, longitude and latitude, meteors, auroras and other night events. Also includes activities dealing with how ancient peoples used the night sky to direct them.

The Reasons for Seasons—A book concerning the order of the earth as well as time and space, and their relationship to the changing seasons. Activities, projects, stories and experiments contribute to an understanding of the seasons and their effect on the earth.

Subject Matter and Teaching Strategy:

The *Brown Paper School Books* may be used as learning experiences for a whole class or small group. They also provide excellent activities for individual enrichment study and for learning centers. The exercises are written for children; thus, little or no teacher intervention is necessary in completing activities.

Rationale:

The authors of this series believe that learning only happens when a child wants to learn. This learning can take place anywhere, and does not require sophisticated teacher aids. These books are designed to motivate a child to want to learn on his own, not only in the classroom, but also at home and at play.

What:	*The Cemetery Box*
	Don Mitchell and Gary Grimm
Published By:	Good Apple, Inc.
	Box 299
	Carthage, Illinois 62321
How To Order:	Order from publisher
	List price: $9.95
	Consumable items:
Description:	One hundred activity cards about "cemetery things"— ghosts, goblins, tombstones, and so on. Designed to provide a wide variety of interesting and imaginative activities for students in grades 4–8; designed for use by individual students or small groups, for several subject areas.
Target Audience:	Intermediate grades.
Materials Provided:	One hundred task cards, a 16 inch by 20 inch foldout, and a "sound sheet."
Subject Matter and Teaching Strategy:	There is a brief introduction and eleven teacher cards to provide ideas for effective utilization of the varius activities in work with gifted children. These cards can be used effectively for project and independent study activities.
Rationale:	These materials are designed to stimulate imaginative skills in students. Students are actively engaged in the use of their imagination.

94

What:	*Creative Activities for the Gifted Child* Lee Bennett Hopkins and Annette F. Shapiro.
Published By:	Fearon Pitman Publishers, Inc. 6 Davis Drive Belmont, California 94002
How To Order:	Order from publisher List price: $2.50

Description:

Many teachers find that they are unable to adequately meet the needs of the individual students in their classrooms due to time limitations. It is often the talented and able child who is left to fend for himself, and so gifted children frequently lack the stimulating environment necessary for their intellectual growth. *Creative Activities for the Gifted Child* was written for the classroom teacher with increasing demands on his or her time. Over 100 easily implemented enrichment ideas are suggested which provide superior students needed teacher guidance while stressing the importance of independent study.

Activities are derived from several educational fields, and the student has the opportunity to work in a variety of environments—the classroom, the school and the community.

The authors have developed activities with the needs of gifted children in mind, including their high level of curiosity as well as their need for achievement. Motivating and stimulating programs which may be developed with suggestions from *Creative Activites for the Gifted Child* will hopefully allow able children to develop beyond the confines of the regular classroom.

Target Audience:

Elementary

Subject Matter and Teaching Strategy:

These activities can be used in connection with language arts, social studies, science and mathematics. They are essentially of an enrichment nature.

Rationale:

The authors assume that supplementary enrichment activities can meet some of the needs of gifted students.

What:	*Creative Expression Books* Scholastic Book Services
Published By:	Scholastic Book Services 901 Sylvan Avenue Englewood Cliffs, New Jersey 07632
How To Order:	Order from publisher. List price: $.60 per book. A free Teaching Guide is included with orders of 10 or more of any title. Consumable items: Individual workbooks.
Description:	Each creative expression book, written to build spelling, vocabulary, grammar, and thinking skills at a particular grade level, consists of fourteen creative writing lessons bound in a colorful, imaginatively designed paperback cover which is not marked for grade level. Each lesson is created to stimulate written expression using a specific technique. Topics covered include parody, detective writing, free verse, cinquains, haiku, descriptive writing, rhymed poetry, and many other types of creative writing. Two basic kinds of lessons are presented. In one kind an explanation of a technique, such as haiku, is followed by examples and pictures for the student to write about. In another type, lesson pictures are presented and the student is asked to write about them in a particular way—for instance, as if he were experiencing the scene pictured. Many of the pictures accompanying the lessons show black and white children in inner-city or urban settings. Topics of current interest such as conversation, overpopulation, and the world food supply are included.
Target Audience:	Grades 2–6.
Materials Provided:	Each of the five workbooks provides space for individual writing in response to each lesson and a page for an individual wordlist. Book titles and grades are the following: *Dinosaur Bones,* grade 2; *Jungle Sounds,* grade 3; *Ghost Ships,* grade 4; *Cook Up Tales,* grade 5; *Adventures with a Three-Spined Stickleback,* Grade 6.

Teacher's Guide:	The teacher's manual for each book provides the rationale for using the workbook and suggests optimum conditions for using the lessons. Discussion ideas are given for each lesson so that the teacher can encourage oral expression. Ideas for follow-up activities are also listed.
Subject Matter and Teaching Strategy:	The content of these lessons is particularly applicable to language arts since lessons involve creative expression, both oral and written, and emphasize creative use of words. The workbooks can be used by a whole class during a writing period or they can be used by small groups or students individually. They would also work well as available material in a learning center.
Rationale:	These workbooks are designed to stimulate exploration and articulation of thoughts and feelings and to encourage creative written and oral expression.

What:	*Creative Expression: Lower Primary* Billy Leon Shumate *Creative Writing: Primary* Billy Leon Shumate *Creative Writing: Intermediate* Alice and Lawrence L. Tomas *Creative Writing: Upper Intermediate* Lawrence L. Tomas
Published By:	Milliken Publishing Company 1100 Research Boulevard St. Louis, Missouri 63132
How To Order:	Order from publisher. List Price: $7.95 for each level. Consumable items: Duplicating masters.
Description:	*Creative Expression* and the three *Creative Writing* books constitute a series designed to stimulate children to think, to detect and express their feelings and attitudes, and to creatively extend what they learn. *Creative Expression* is designed for those without writing skills, and accordingly requires oral responding. The other books of the series concentrate on creative expression through writing. Colorful transparencies that entertain and hold the attention of children are central to the books. Duplicating masters of activity pages ask opinions and invite creative answers about the situations depicted. Creative writing suggestions are included in the upper levels, with thematic pictures provided in the lower primary booklet.
Target Audience:	Lower Primary to Upper Intermediate.
Materials Provided:	8 ½″ × 11″ color transparencies of discussion themes and situations for use on overhead projectors. (Booklets are available without transparencies.) Duplicating masters provide individual facsimiles of transparencies for each student's personal use.
Teacher's Guide:	The teacher's guide gives objectives for each unit, suggested questions, and additional activities.

Subject Matter and Teaching Strategy:	Themes for each unit are of everyday activities, special events, fantasy, animals, and other subjects that are interesting to the child and can stimulate his or her thinking. The series may be useful as an occasional addition to normal classroom work or as a regular part of the class activities. Students can use the activities individually and progress as they desire.
Rationale:	Emphasis is placed on encouraging the child to express himself and his ideas, while grading and criticism are de-emphasized. Individual differences are recognized and accounted for, and the importance of the recognition of and the expression of each child's individuality is stressed.

What:	*Creative Language Projects: Independent Activities in Lanauge Arts* (Books A-E) Mary Pat Mullaney
Published By:	Milliken Publishing Company 1100 Research Boulevard St. Louis, Missouri 63132
How To Order:	Order from publisher. List price: $4.25 per booklet. Consumable items: Each booklet contains 28 duplicating masters.
Description:	*Creative Language Projects* requires students to think creatively, use their imagination, think of unusual ideas, and solve unusual problems. The individual problems are meant to be fun and give children practice in expressing themselves in a creative manner through original writing, evaluation, and problem solving.
Target Audience:	Book A, Grades 1–2. Book B, Grades 2–3. Book C, Grades 3–4. Book D, Grades 4–5. Book E, Grades 5–6.
Materials Provided:	Includes 8 ½″ × 11″ duplicating masters (28 per book) of illustrations and related questions that require opinion, problem solving, and creative expression of the child's own thoughts about the problems and situations presented.
Teacher's Guide:	Booklets are prefaced by an explanation of the exercises and how the teacher may best use them.
Subject Matter and Teaching Strategy:	The exercises that comprise each booklet concern everyday objects, animals, and people with whom the child should be familiar. The materials may be used as supplements to regular reading or English programs, for extra credit, or for whatever specialized purpose the teacher desires. The projects may be most useful when a more informal fun atmosphere is desired in the classroom.
Rationale:	Emphasis is placed on the individual nature of each child's creative processes and abilities. Through individual use of the activity sheet replications, children can find their own answers and express themselves in relation to ideas, objects, and events common to their own world.

100

What:	*Creative Teaching Press Materials*
Published By:	Creative Teaching Press, Inc. 5305 Production Dr. Huntington Beach, California 92649
How To Order:	Order from publisher List price: Varies with materials purchased Consumable items: None
Description:	Creative Teaching Press publishes materials designed to provide supplementary enrichment in a wide variety of curricular areas. Activities go beyond traditional classroom lessons, and deal wtih topics in a creative and individualized manner.
Target Audience:	Grades 1–8, depending on material.
Materials Provided:	Some of the Creative Teaching Press materials include:

Bright Ideas (Grades 4–8)—This book provides a collection of lessons and activities for supplementary enrichment in the elementary classroom. The eleven chapters include: photography, publishing, poetry, tower of self, geometric line drawing, weaving, machines, the law, body fat, the heart at work, and blood pressure. $6.95

Keys to Understanding Mankind (Grades 4–12)—This is a set of reading-oriented, open-ended activities. There are 55 keys that unlock an idca about man in relation to himself and others. Each key idea is followed by a list of activities which guide children in investigating the idea. For each idea there is an illustration which expresses the thinking structure involved in the idea. Some of the key ideas are the following: There is a reason for all behavior; every issue has two sides; and courage can be defined. $5.95

Let's Begin (Preprimary)—*Let's Begin* is a collection of over 100 creative ideas of interesting, stimulating, and enjoyable activities that stimulate the expression and imagination of young children. The ideas are indexed into areas of art, mathematics, language and literature, movement education, science, and social relationships. The activities range from finger painting to storytelling to block-building, and involve classroom work, dancing, nature, trips, and interpersonal situations. Each idea is described on a card that outlines materials, procedures, and suggestions. In some cases, related books for the teacher and child are listed. $6.95

Search and Research (Grades 1–3)—These are packages of task cards designed to introduce primary aged children to research and information-gathering skills. Set A contains 50 task cards with activities dealing with alphabetical order, classification, directions, resource people, TV, signs, maps, phone book, newspaper, dictionary, and library. Set B includes 48 cards with activities on using pictures, using maps, using classification, using the encyclopedia, and using what you know. $4.95

Story Starters (Set 1—intermediate elementary; Set 2—primary elementary)—*Story Starters* suggest 50 illustrated ideas that interest and motivate students to express themselves creatively. Each Story Starter card presents an interesting situation that the child can write about and extend. The subjects that are dealt with are those that are most stimulating and relevant to the experiences and imagination of young children. Many involve adventure and fantasy and require good use of the imagination. Some of the subjects involved are buried treasure, castles, sports, and animals. $4.95

Think-Ins (Grades 4–12)—This is a series of 30 task cards that provide ideas and suggestions to stimulate creative thinking and problem solving. Each card is on a different topic that concerns mankind and his environment, and presents a challenge, things to think about, suggestions for activities, plus ideas for further inquiry. Sample topics are propaganda, education, overpopulation, garbage, and health. The problems that are presented in the challenge are to be solved through the processes described in the sections that follow. Hypothesizing, researching, discovering facts, and drawing conclusions are some of the processes that the student practices and should learn from the program. $6.95

Subject Matter and Teaching Strategy:	Creative Teaching Press materials cover a wide range of subjects, but tend to emphasize language arts and creativity development. Most activity kits and books are especially amenable to individual student study. Students can work at their own pace and can find activities of interest to them.
Rationale:	Creative Teaching Press materials are based on the concept that students working on their own on areas of special interest find their studies more enjoyable and rewarding. Activities which encourage children to investigate and discover aid in developing expressive and thinking abilities.

What:	*Creative Teaching Series*
Published By:	Allyn and Bacon, Inc. 470 Atlantic Avenue Boston, Massachusetts
How To Order:	Order from publisher. List price: Range from $8.95–$12.95. Paperback and cloth versions of most books. Consumable items: None.
Description:	The *Creative Teaching Series* is comprised of seven books concerned with creative teaching in the elementary schools. Each book contains methods and activities that promote creativity in the classroom. Seven different areas are covered: language arts, reading and literature, art, music, social studies, mathematics, and science.
Target Audience:	Grade levels 1–8.
Materials Provided:	*Creative Teaching of the Language Arts in the Elementary School* (2nd Edition) offers methods for creativity in the language arts. Areas covered by the book include listening, oral expression, creative writing, handwriting, grammar, word usage, and spelling.

Creative Teaching of Reading in the Elementary School (2nd Edition) presents principles of creative development in reading and literature and ways teachers can use these principles in the classroom. Reading in the primary and intermediate grades, literature, and poetry are covered in this book.

Creative Teaching of Art in the Elementary School is the third book of the series. Methods for supporting creativity through art are described.

Creative Teaching of the Social Studies in the Elementary School Second Edition, offers techniques for nurturing creativity in the social studies. The book discusses the use of textbooks, audiovisual methods, individualization, buzz groups, brainstorming, and various other methods.

Creative Teaching of Music in the Elementary School offers a variety of techniques to foster creativity through the music program.

Creative Teaching of Mathematics in the Elementary School Second Edition, presents ways of teaching mathematics creatively. Addition, subtraction, multiplication, and fractions are some of the areas covered in the book.

Creative Teaching of Science in the Elementary School (2nd Edition) is the final book of the series. It deals with methods which foster creativity in science.

Teacher's Guide: Each book is designed as instructional material for teachers.

Subject Matter and Teaching Strategy: Each of the eight books covers a different subject area. Teachers can easily take the principles of creative teaching which are presented and adapt them to their own classrooms.

Rationale: The ideas and principles presented in the books are designed as guidelines for creative teaching in the elementary school. Each book proposes to build favorable attitudes towards creative teaching rather than to develop a "cookbook" of teaching methodology.

What:	*Creative Writing Skills* (Book I and Book II) C.M. Charles and M. Church
Published *By:*	T.S. Denison and Company, Inc. 9601 Newton Avenue, S. Minneapolis, Minnesota 55431
How *To* *Order:*	Order from publisher. List price: Book I (No. 513–0077–8)@$4.95 each. Student Workbook (No. 513–00180–8)@$.95 each. Book II (No. 513–00179–4)@$4.95 each. Student Workbook (No. 513–00178–6)@$.95 each. Consumable items: Workbooks.

Description: *Creative Writing Skills* (I and II) offers the elementary school teacher a series of easy to teach writing exercises which develop creative writing skills. Each series of exercises was designed to increase the generation and flow of ideas from children and to develop skills of putting these new ideas into language. Each series of lessons emphasizes *thought,* rather than handwriting, punctuation, grammar, or capitalization. These latter skills should be developed in the language curriculum. This program offers writing activities which can augment and supplement the present language curriculum in important ways.

Creative Writing Skills (I and II) seems to achieve these four specific goals: (1) to improve the child's ability to select words and phrases that are appropriate to a situation, (2) to develop organization skills incidentally through purposeful writing acitivities, (3) to teach children how to write reasonable, coherent, possible, and satisfying endings, and (4) to encourage unusual and exciting beginnings to their compositions. Each lesson concentrates on developing particular components of a composition (i.e., main ideas, supporting ideas, topic sentences, sequence, paragraphing) rather than entire compositions. The lessons were designed to be taught in their proposed sequence. However, the lessons are internally flexible enough to be modified to suit the needs of the class.

Target
Audience: *Creative Writing Skills* (Book I) is designed for use in grades K–3. *Creative Writing Skills* (Book II) is designed for use in grades 4–6.

106

Materials Provided:	The *Creative Writing Skills* program consists of a *teacher's manual and a student workbook*. The student workbook contains pictures and writing space which correspond to the various lessons described in the teacher's manual.
Teacher's Guide:	The guidebook for teaching creative writing skills describes and explains the *Creative Writing Skills* program. The time for each writing exercise is given. The purpose and goal of the lessons are described. Procedures for the activity are explained and suggestions on how to make "the most efficient use of the lessons" are also given.

A copy of the student workbook is attached to the teacher's guidebook. |
| *Subject Matter and Teaching Strategy:* | *Creative Writing Skills* (Books I and II) are designed for use as a supplement to the regular composition curriculum. Mechanics of writing is not stressed explicitly. The program emphasizes activities which increase the generation and flow of ideas and the development of writing skills for putting these new ideas on paper rather than skills of handwriting, punctuation, grammar, or capitalization.

Each writing activity can be effectively performed by the entire class for periods of 25–30 minutes. They will be most effective if separated by no more than two days between lessons. Although the program is designed to develop a particular skill in a systematic, sequential way, each lesson is internally flexible enough to be modified to meet the needs of the class. |
| *Rationale:* | *Creative Writing Skills* (Book I and II) is based upon the rationale that no matter what the backgrounds of children are, they can learn to think more creatively and write more effectively. The exercises in this program were designed to make each child a better communicator. Skills of communication are very important and generally can be developed only with practice. This writing program attempts to inspire children to create novel ideas and to provide guidance in ways to write more effectively. |

What:	*Developing Thinking Skills* Hollis Griffin
Published By:	Frank Schaffer Publications, Inc. 26616 Indian Peak Rd. Palos Verdes Peninsula, California 90274
How To Order:	Order from publisher List price: $4.25 Consumable items: None
Description:	Activities covering a wide range of subject areas aid students in improving their thinking abiliites. "Extra" assignments are provided at the end of each activity, allowing highly motivated students to study areas of interest in greater depth. Research skills are emphasized as well as cognitive abilities.
Target Audience:	Grades 3–6.
Materials Provided:	One book of 34 pull-out pages which are easily reproduced for use with individual students.
Subject Matter and Teaching Strategy:	*Developing Thinking Skills* is designed for use by individual students. Children are self-directed throughout the activities, and therefore teacher preparation and instruction are minimal. The activities could be used in the language arts area and in teaching research skills.
Rationale:	Individual activities that are motivating to students will aid in developing the belief that learning can be fun. Children who eagerly anticipate thinking exercises may be expected to learn more and remember what they have learned longer.

What:	*Disney's Let's Write A Story*
Published By:	Disney Schoolhouse 500 S. Buena Vista Street Burbank, California 91521
How To Order:	Order from publisher List price: $5.95 Consumable items: 24 duplicating masters per book.
Description:	*Disney's Let's Write A Story* books provide language arts experiences through the use of familiar and motivating Disney characters. Activities help cultivate creative writing skills while also building basic language arts concepts.
Target Audience:	Book I—Grades 1–3 Book II—Grades 4–6
Materials Provided:	Each book contains 24 duplicating masters.
Teacher's Guide:	At the top of each page are listed the skills and concepts covered on that page. A summary is also provided at the beginning of each book which provides an overview of concepts, skills and activities by page number.
Subject Matter and Teaching Strategy:	Language arts skills to be developed include vocabulary, spelling, punctuation, and creative writing (fantasy, humor, science fiction, description, reporting). Activities are designed to engage students in high level thinking, and introduce children to such literary elements as plot, theme, character, setting, dialogue, and point of view. Teacher use of the books is flexible; pages may be used for entire class instruction, learning centers, independent study, or enrichment activities.
Rationale:	Creative writing activities are best fostered in a stimulating yet not wholly unfamiliar atmosphere. Likewise, the development of basic language arts skills can be tedious and boring for students if a motivating climate is not provided. *Disney's Let's Write A Story* aids in building creative expression and promotes enthusiasm for the learning of basic concepts through the use of motivating Disney characters.

What:	*Educational Insight Boxes*
Published By:	Educational Insights, Inc. 20435 S. Tillman Avenue Carson, California 90746
How To Order:	Order from publisher. List price: $5.95–$6.95 Consumable items: Optional student workbooks.
Description:	*Educational Insights Boxes* offer exciting exercises in creative thinking for elementary school children. Games, activities, and skill builders are written on separate index cards; dividers for different sections are provided; the box doubles as a file. Boxes for five subject areas are available.
Target Audience:	Grades 1–6.
Materials Provided:	*The Language Arts Box* ($6.95) consists of 150 games, activities and skill builders. The lower grade level activities are found at the beginning of each section. There are eleven sections which include creative writing, organization aids for creative writing, manipulations, public speaking, dramatics, radio and television, informational writings, development, and parts of speech. *Elementary Science Experiments* ($6.95) consists of 135 experiments and activities. It contains twelve different sections dealing with magnetism, electricity, air, aerophysics, simple machines, weather, heat, water, chemistry, sound, light, and extra material. Students workbooks, at $3.50 each, and a teacher's edition at $3.95 are available from publisher. *The Art Box* ($6.95) contains creative art activities for the intermediate grades. Four different sections include a general introduction, behavioral objectives, two-dimensional activities, and three-dimensional activities. *Write On!* ($5.95) is a collection of 70 creative writing ideas and teacher techniques. The different sections deal with a writer's workshop, motivators, word power, flair for fantasy, holiday happenings, and potpourri.

Mind Expanders ($6.95) consists of challenging activities designed primarily for gifted students. They are to be used individually by the student. Six different areas are covered: math, creative writing, art, social studies, poetry and book reports, and science.

Social Studies Strategies ($6.95) contains 140 activities for improving social studies teaching and learning processes. The six sections include dramatic play and role playing, stimulating games, social studies games, maps and globes, miscellaneous map experiences, and manipulative experiences and the social studies.

Magnetism and Electricity ($5.95) is a box of 50 activities and experiments covering facts and concepts related to magnetism and electricity. Experiments follow an inquiry approach. Side one of each card is organized into three categories: Question or Activity, Background, and Experiment; on side two are Observations, Conclusion, and some Head Stretchers. Cards may be used individually for enrichment activities or by an entire class as a unit of study.

Finding Your Roots ($5.95) is not a box of activities, but a book of duplication masters designed to be highly motivating to students learning research and writing skills. Students use research techniques to study their own lives and backgrounds. Writing experience is provided and students share their research findings and experiences with others.

Teacher's Guide:

Each box contains an index card directed to the teacher. This card presents a general overview of the box and the activities provided.

Subject Matter and Teaching Strategy:

The activities, games, and skill builders can be used to supplement a classroom presentation of a subject area. The group as a whole may engage in the exercises, or each child can work independently. A teacher may expand the box by adding new activities.

Rationale:

The boxes offer creative and inviting activities. These activities provide students an opportunity to think and discover, and in this way increase their knowledge of the subject area and their creative-thinking abilities.

What:	*Fact, Fantasy and Folklore*
	Greta B. Lipson and Baxter Morrison
Published By:	Good Apple, Inc.
	Box 299
	Carthage, Illinois 62321
How To Order:	Order from publisher
	List price: $9.95
	Consumable items: None

Description: This ingenious book consists of eleven folk tales and related activities for use in language arts classes. One significant issue has been identified for each story, and students are shown a different perspective on the story and the issue, thus requiring them to see alternative sides to a problem. The book is designed to develop skills in reading, writing, listening, oral expression, and valuing and to foster critical thinking.

Target Audience: Grades 3–12

Materials Provided: One *Fact, Fantasy and Folklore* book

Subject Matter and Teaching Strategy: Although *Fact, Fantasy and Folklore* is specifically designed for use in language arts, the teacher may take an interdisciplinary approach by considering other areas, such as social studies, as well. Students read and discuss the tales, and are encouraged to challenge the conventional acceptance of an issue. Besides stimulating critical discussion, each unit contains such activities as role playing and improvisational drama. The teacher is provided with background clues to aid him or her in developing major lesson plans.

Rationale: Looking at stories from a new perspective invites divergent thinking and imagination building. Understanding a different approach to everyday values is fun for students and, at the same time, aids greatly in developing creative thought, especially flexibility.

What:	*Famous Black People in American History*
Published By:	Edu-Cards Division of Binney and Smith Easton, Pennsylvania 18042
How To Order:	Order from publisher List price: Write publisher. Consumable items: None
Description:	*Famous Black People in American History* is a set of 36 self-study cards dealing with the role of the Black American in shaping the history of the United States. In flash-card fashion, side one has a picture of the eminent individual, and side two gives a brief synopsis of the person's accomplishments.
Target Audience:	Grades 4–8
Materials Provided:	Thirty-six flash cards on sturdy cardboard
Teacher's Guide:	An instruction booklet is included with the set of cards. This guide lists all persons described in the set and suggests possible games and quizzes for class use.
Subject Area and Teaching Strategy:	The cards are appropriate for use in social studies lessons, specifically United States history. The teacher should give students an opportunity to read the cards and study the pictures. After learning the information, students should be able to associate the famous person with his or her contribution and period of history. Oral and written quiz games are described for use in small groups or with the entire class. Quiz questions are also included.
Rationale:	The purpose of these cards is to develop an increased understanding on the part of teachers and students of the contributions made by blacks in all areas throughout America's history. The cards also provide a good starting point for further individual study of the famous people.

What:	*Frank Schaffer Activity Cards*
Published By:	Frank Schaffer Publications, Inc. 26616 Indian Peak Road Palos Verdes Peninsula, California 90274
How To Order:	Order from publisher List price: $5.50 each Comsumable items: None
Description:	*Frank Schaffer Activity Cards* cover virtually every area of educational interest to the teacher in an entertaining and motivating manner to students. Cards are printed on sturdy paper and may be easily removed from each book for individual or group use.
Target Audience:	Grades 1–6, depending on card set
Materials Provided:	Each book of activity cards may be purchased individually. Some of the books are described below:

Career Exploration: Activities are geared toward acquainting students with a wide variety of occupations and suggest research projects for students to delve more deeply into areas of interest. Suggested uses of cards include career centers, discussions, debates, and role-playing.

Creative Writing: Cards provide students with motivating stimuli to encourage creative writing. Activities include the writing of sentences, stories, directions, advertisements, newspapers, poems and autobiographies.

Book Reporting: Activities and projects are designed to encourage children to share books they read in original and creative ways. Sample exercises include writing a diary, providing a new ending to a story, making a filmstrip, interviewing characters, and holding a trial to describe the book.

Read and Reason: Cards help develop vocabulary and word attack skills, aiding students in becoming more fluent and flexible in their oral and written language. Activities include sentence building, use of the dictionary, homonyms, scrambled words and sentences, and idioms.

Subject
Matter
and
Teaching
Strategy:

Cards are reproducible so that each student may have his own copy to work with. Sets of cards may also be used to set up learning centers for group activities.

Rationale:

Gifted children in the regular classroom need independent enrichment activities to prevent boredom from setting in. *Frank Schaffer's Activity Cards* help the busy teacher provide stimulating exercises in several subject areas with little preparation time necessary on the part of the teacher.

What:	*The Good Apple Creative Writing Book* Gary Grimm and Don Mitchell
Published By:	Good Apple, Inc. Box 299 Carthage, Illinois 62321
How To Order:	Order from publisher List price: $6.95 Comsumable items: None
Description:	*The Good Apple Creative Writing Book* provides children with the opportunity to increase their creative thinking and writing skills through the use of divergent and evaluative activities in a format which is practical, easy-to-use and reasonably priced.
Target Audience:	Grades 3–6
Materials Provided:	One *Creative Writing Book*
Subject Matter and Teaching Strategy:	The activities are designed to provide teachers and students with alternative approaches to creative writing, emphasizing that flexibility is a necessary component in developing creative writing abilities. Several relevant topics are suggested, such as magazine interviews, advertisements, autobiographies, a symbol dictionary and travel brochures, to teach practical concepts of current interest to students in a creative and imaginative fashion.
Rationale:	Most classroom materials give first priority to the development of convergent thinking skills. The authors of *The Good Apple Creative Writing Book* believe that divergent and evaluative thinking abilities are equally important to the educational process, but are often ignored. These skills may be more important than the more logical, fact-finding process of convergent thinking to help students meet their continually changing environments.

What:	*Good Apple Records*
Published By:	Good Apple, Inc. Box 299 Carthage, Illinois 62321
How To Order:	Order from publisher List Price: $6.95 each record, $5.95 each book. Consumable items: None
Description:	Good Apple Records combines appealing children's songs with divergent activities to stimulate the creative thinking skills of fluency, flexibility, originality, and elaboration.
Target Audience:	Grades Kindergarten–6
Materials Provided:	One Good Apple record plus one activity book per set. Record ($6.95) and book ($5.95) sets include: *Dandy-Lions Never Roar*, by Joe Wayman and Don Mitchell: This album stresses divergent thinking and self-concept building through such songs as "Spiders, Bugs 'n Snakes" and "I Have Feelings." Large group brainstorming activities and individual exercises that relate to each song are provided. *Anything Can Happen*, by Joe Wayman: This record also emphasizes creativity development with the title song, "Because It's Fuzzy," "What Would You Be?" and others. Side 2 of the record suggests activities to introduce and follow up songs. *Imagination and Me*, by Joe Wayman and Don Mitchell: This album explores the potential for imagination that rests in every child. Self concept is also stressed through, "I Like Me" and "If You Think You Can or If You Think You Can't, You're Absolutely Right."
Teacher's Guide:	The activity book provided with each record explains creativity and discusses examples of fluency, flexibility, originality, and elaboration. Several pages offer suggested activities to use with the records for further creativity stimulation.

Subject
Matter
and
Teaching
Strategy:

Development of creative thinking in students as well as self-concept building are the aims of the records.

Teaching strategies are flexible. The authors suggest possible plans for class use. The first days of a new song involve listening to, singing and dancing with and discussing the song. Teachers may then duplicate pages from the activity book corresponding with the song, and the following days may involve working on activities and sharing results.

Rationale:

Music is a natural motivator to all children. By using music as an aid to imagination development, children become more creative and spontaneous in their thoughts and actions.

What:	*Imagination Express: Saturday Subway Ride* Gary R. Davis and Gerald DiPego
Published By:	DOK Publishers, Inc. 71 Radcliffe Road Buffalo, New York 14215
How To Order:	Order from publisher. List price: $3.95. Consumable items: Detachable master maker sheets to be used with spirit masters or mimeo stencils.
Description:	The *Imagination Express: Saturday Subway Ride* is an imaginative 92-page workbook in a travel story-exercise format designed to teach creative-thinking techniques and positive attitudes toward creativity. Pupils buy a ticket for the Imagination Express by paying with a song or story or whatever other imaginative thing each can create and then it is "All Aboard" for a wild, fun-filled adventure which takes him from Kansas City to Pittsburg to Dublin to Tokyo to Santa Monica and back. Just like Alice in Wonderland, the pupil will meet strange and wonderful people and places, experience the fun of creating fantastic happenings and solve interesting problems in the *Saturday Subway Ride*.
Target Audience:	The workbook was specifically designed to be used over a two-to-four month period with intermediate (3–8) grade level pupils.
Materials Provided:	One story booklet. This booklet contains seven stories based upon an imaginative subway ride from Kansas to Dublin and back again.
	Eighteen Master Sheets. These detachable sheets provide exercises in flexible, fluent and elaborative thinking which are used in conjunction with the story booklet.
Teacher's Guide:	*Imagination Express* is intended to be a "point of departure" for elementary grade teachers to begin a new kind of thinking about instructional planning and materials. *Imagination Express* is a valuable resource of ideas for the enthusiastic teacher in fostering creativity in students.

Subject
Matter
and
Teaching
Strategy:

Imagination Express provides practice in verbal expression and in creative writing. The story theme is an around-the-world subway ride with fantastic episodes at each stop, some of which are supplied by the pupil.

Throughout the course of the journey, the pupil is encouraged to demonstrate his understanding of five creative problem-solving techniques by means of the pertinent workbook exercises presented throughout the text. The student learns to identify important attributes or parts of an object, considering each attribute as a source of potential improvement. Students consider each item on a prepared list as a possible source of innovation with respect to a given problem. By means of a metaphorical activity, students are asked to consider how other people, animals, and plants solve a similar problem. Groups of students use the "brainstorming" technique to find solutions for problems such as "how to turn a classroom into a foreign planet."

The practice activities given in the workbook should help pupils develop verbal fluency and imaginative writing skills.

Rationale:

The *Imagination Express: Saturday Subway Ride* was intended to stimulate the creative problem-solving ability of pupils by fostering a favorable predisposition toward "wild" or imaginative ideas. It is possible to learn to be a more productive and more original thinker by focusing upon the development of strategies of thinking which facilitate the generation of ideas. A child's creative ability can be improved through practice with the techniques of generating new ideas.

The creative development of children depends largely upon the sensitivity and imagination of teachers and curriculum developers. *Imagination Express* encourages the teacher to find new and different experiences for children.

What:	*I See/I Think I See* Illa Podendorf and Jeffery Benson
Published By:	Ideal School Supply Co. 11000 S. Lavergne Avenue Oak Lawn, Illinois 60453
How To Order:	Order from publisher (No. 5661) List price: $4.95 Consumable items: Ditto masters
Description:	These materials are part of a series entitled, "Experiences in Process Learning." The objectives of the activities include: (1) identifying observations and inferences: (2) distinguishing between observations and inferences: and (3) constructing alternate inferences.
Target Audience:	Primary
Materials Provided:	The set includes a folder for the teacher, four ditto masters, and approximately forty printed cards with pictures to utilize with the activities.
Teacher's Guide:	There is a four page printed teacher's guide which gives suggestions for using the activities.
Subject Matter and Teaching Strategy:	*I See/I Think I See* focuses on critical thinking and inquiry processes. The material is especially useful in science instruction with young children.
Rationale:	The authors designed these activities to be independent learning units for young children. They stress thinking processes which are relevant in science education.

What:	*Keys to Understanding Mankind* Edited by Sandra Nina Kaplan and Jo Ann Butom Kaplan
Published By:	Creative Teaching Press 5305 Production Dr. Huntington Beach, California 92649
How To Order:	Order from publisher. List price: $5.95. Consumable items: None.

Description:

    Keys to Understanding Mankind is a set of reading-oriented, open-ended activities. There are 55 Keys that unlock an idea about man in relation to himself and others. Each key idea is followed by a list of activities which guide children in investigating the idea. For each idea there is an illustration which expresses the thinking structure involved in the idea. Some of the key ideas are the following: There is a reason for all behavior; Every issue has two sides; and Courage can be defined.

    The directing activities suggest using the characters and elements of stories to demonstrate the ideas and investigate them.

Target Audience:

Grades 4–12.

Materials Provided:

Fifty-five keys on heavy paper.
Teacher's Guide.

Teacher's Guide:

    The kit is introduced by a statement of the objectives of the series. There are suggestions for the teacher that include an explanation of the use of the cards.

Subject Matter and Teaching Strategy:

    The *Keys* may be useful in the classroom as a way of interpreting assigned reading material or as a basis for extra-credit work. A single card can be assigned to one student, to small groups, or to an entire class.

    When kept in a learning center, the series serves as an enrichment program in language arts or social sciences.

Rationale:

    Keys to Understanding Mankind is based upon the belief that by encouraging students to investigate and discover, their individual expressive and thinking abilities can be developed and enhanced.

What:	*Kids' Stuff*
Published By:	Incentive Publications, Inc. P. O. Box 120189 Nashville, Tennessee 37212
How To Order:	Order from publisher List price: See each title. Consumable items: None
Description:	Kids' Stuff books offers creative and challenging exercise in several curricular areas. The pages in each book are attractive and stimulating and they encourage children to open their minds and think.
Target Audience:	Grades 1–6, depending on the book used.
Materials Provided:	Each book may be purchased separately for use in a particular subject area. Listed below are several of the books available.

Kids' Stuff—Reading and Language Experiences (Primary): Intended for use as supplementary enrichment to established language arts programs, this book provides creative reading and spelling activities designed to develop early language arts skills. The book includes both descriptions of activities for the teacher and pages of motivating exercises which may be duplicated for student use. $10.95.

Kids' Stuff—Math: This book offers fresh ideas for the teacher to use in promoting student interest in mathematics. Activities, games, and learning centers are included, with each exercise designed to fit a specific math skill. An appendix provides a complete list of elementary math skills as well as a glossary of math terms, symbols, formulas and measures. Activity pages may be duplicated for classroom usage. $10.95.

Pumpkins, Pinwheels and Peppermint Packages: Open-ended learning center activities which deal with special days or seasons of the year are the focus of this book. Each special occasion section includes activities in communications, creative arts, environmental awareness, and mathematics. Pages may be duplicated, and the authors suggest presenting activities in free choice interest centers to stimulate differing student interests. A Teacher's Edition is also available to aid the teacher in designing creative classroom activities. Teacher's Edition, $10.95, Student Edition, $7.95.

Nooks, Crannies and Corners: This book is aimed specifically at the teacher, administrator or parent for use in designing individualized learning centers. Defining, developing and creating activities for centers are all discussed at length, and examples of activities and ways to implement them are abundant. $6.95.

Kids' Stuff—Social Studies: This book provides an interesting variety of activities for the social studies program. Many of the activities stress creative thinking and problem solving. $10.95.

Teacher's Guide:

Kids' Stuff books include a section suggesting possible uses of activities. Most books are geared toward the teacher, devoting most of their time to explaining creative ideas for use in stimulating subject area learning. They also include student pages for duplicating.

Subject Matter and Teaching Strategy:

Subject matter depends on the book, with all major curricular areas covered.

Teachers are encouraged to use the books as supplemental enrichment activities to regular classroom lessons. Adaptations for use in learning centers is easy and helps meet individual student needs and interests.

Rationale:

Students approach elementary skills areas with varying interests and needs. Individualized and open ended activities are important in developing the basic skill areas and in promoting enthusiasm for learning. *Kids' Stuff* books provide creative activities and stimulate teachers to design interesting classroom exercises of their own.

What:	*Learning Through Creative Thinking* and *Mathematics Through Creative Thinking* M. Ann Dirkes
Published By:	DOK Publishers, Inc. 71 Radcliffe Road Buffalo, New York 14214
How To Order:	Order from publisher List price: $3.95 per packet Consumable items: None
Description:	*Learning Through Creative Thinking* and *Mathematics Through Creative Thinking* are activity packets designed to develop divergent thinking powers and, as a result, increase student intellectual abilities and affective growth.
Target Audience:	Grades 3–6
Materials Provided:	*Learning Through Creative Thinking*—Teacher's guide, introduction and instructions for students, 70 activity cards. *Mathematics Through Creative Thinking*—Teacher's guide, introduction and instructions for students, 51 activity cards.
Teacher's Guide:	Discusses cognitive and affective objectives of the activity cards and suggests ways to implement the cards in the classroom. Activities which foster specific abilities are also presented for the teacher. Lists of possible responses to several activities may be found in the back of this booklet. These activities can be made available to students as activities are completed.
Subject Matter and Teaching Strategy:	Although *Learning Through Creative Thinking* and *Mathematics Through Creative Thinking* deal with different subject areas by means of subject specific activities, both sets of cards attempt to provide for basically the same end goals: the development of intellectual abilities, the promotion of learning in specific subject areas, and the cultivation of affective development. More specific objectives include the development of divergent production and evaluative abilities as well as problem solving techniques. The activity cards are beneficial for use with academically and creatively gifted students in that children are aided in learning and inquiring independently.

Several factors may be varied in implementing the programs. Cards may be used with all students in the class or only the academically and/or creatively gifted. Students may do activities alone, in small groups, or in large groups (although emphasis is on independent activity). Activities may be used in a learning center, as a substitute for more routine teaching, or at home as the student has free time. Other variables include feedback, monitoring, materials use, and sequence.

Students are directed to complete activities one through five within a few days. These cards teach brainstorming techniques which are used throughout the activities. After activity #5, students may work on cards out of sequence (in *Learning Through Creative Thinking*, students are requested to work through activity #13 before working out of sequence.)

Student troubleshooters are identified by the teacher and children may turn to them if they run into difficulties. Students ask for teacher aid only if the troubleshooter is unable to help.

Rationale: School curriculums are usually designed to facilitate lower level skills such as memorization of facts and concepts and understanding of concepts. Emphasis is most often on convergent production. In mathematics and in general learning, stress is placed less on problem solving and divergent responses, and more on arriving at one correct solution with little regard for the integrative processes of learning. These two programs were developed to cultivate cognitive skills and subject matter learning through the use of divergent thinking strategies which allow the child to learn continuously and on his own, utilizing high level thinking strategies.

What	*Let's Begin*
	Doris Edmund
Published By:	Creative Teaching Press
	5305 Production Drive
	Huntington Beach, California 92649
How To Order:	Order from publisher.
	List price: $5.95.
	Consumable items: None.

Description: *Let's Begin* is a collection of over 100 creative ideas of interesting, stimulating, and enjoyable activities that stimulate the expression and imagination of young children. The ideas are indexed into areas of art, mathematics, language and literature, movement education, science, and social relationships. The activities range from finger painting to storytelling to blockbuilding, and involve classroom work, dancing, nature, trips, and interpersonal situations.

      Each idea is described on a card that outlines materials, procedures, and suggestions. In some cases, related books for the teacher and child are listed.

Target Audience: Preprimary.

Materials Provided: Over 100 4″ × 5″ index cards of ideas, indexed and collected in a file box.

Teacher's Guide.

Teacher's Guide: Each category of ideas is introduced with an explanation of the objectives of the activities and hints to the teacher on how to promote the expressive creativity and learning of the children through the use of the ideas.

Subject Matter and Teaching Strategy: A wide variety of activities is offered, including games, songs, and dances. The general course of activity in the preprimary classroom is not generally based on written material, and the *Let's Begin* activities are correspondingly geared towards nonwritten performance. The ideas are oriented towards varying levles of ability, and the teacher may discover that it is best to involve separate groups in different activities geared to children's readiness. Some activities may occupy the whole class, such as dramatic presentations and singing.

The *Let's Begin* series can serve as an enriching extension of a regular daily program, or an entire program may be built around the expressive activities that it contains.

Rationale: The rationale underlying *Let's Begin* is that the expressive involvement of young children in their learning is very important. By encouraging children to explore, observe, question, and express themselves, learning becomes fruitful and rewarding for both teacher and pupil. The author demonstrates the conviction that an interested, enthusiastic, and warm teacher who is supportive of the individuality of the student, can facilitate the full growth of each individual.

What:	*The Month-to-Month Me* Linda Schwartz
Published By:	The Learning Works P.O. Box 6187 Santa Barbara, California 93111
How To Order:	Order from publisher List price: $4.50 Consumable items: None
Description:	*The Month-to-Month Me* contains 40 activities which enable students to keep an ongoing journal about themselves. Exercises are divided into months, with 4 activities per month for the school year.
Target Audience:	Grades 2–6
Materials Provided:	One *Month-to-Month Me* book
Subject Matter and Teaching Strategy:	Affective learning is the main emphasis of *Month-to-Month Me*. Through the course of a school year students gain insight into themselves and their feelings by use of the activities in the book. Exercises also develop creative thinking, writing and arts skills. Activities may be reproduced for individual students, and are well suited to independent work and use in learning centers. It is suggested that students make a book out of the activities at the end of the year.
Rationale:	By continuously working on activities throughout the school year, students gain self-awareness while constantly building self concepts. At the end of the year, children have a meaningful remembrance of themselves during the school year, reflecting their on-going emotional and creative growth.

What:	*New Directions in Creativity* Mark A,B,I,II,III, 1976 Joseph S. Renzulli, Linda Smith, Barbara Ford, Mary Jo Renzulli
Published By:	Harper & Row, Publisher, Inc. School Department 2500 Crawford Avenue Evanston, Illinois 60201
How To Order:	Order from publisher. List price: $20.00 Consumable items: Each book contains 48 duplicating masters of activities.
Description:	*New Directions in Creativity* is designed to develop the creative thinking skills of children through exercises in divergent thinking. The programs concentrate on improving fluency, flexibility, originality, and elaboration in the context of language arts through making up stories and sentences and working with words in a variety of ways.
Target Audience:	No rigid grade levels are prescribed, but grades K–3 for Mark A and B and grades 4–8 for Mark I, II and III are most highly recommended.

Mark A	*Grades Kindergarten—1*
Mark B	*Grades 2–3*
Mark I	*Grades 4–5*
Mark II	*Grades 5–6*
Mark III	*Grades 6–7*

Materials Provided:	Each level (Mark A,B,I,II,III) consists of a book containing a teacher's guide and 48 duplicating masters.
Teacher's Guide:	The Teacher's Guide presents a description of the history, purpose, and goals of the program. Also included is a summary of some of the theory and research that led to the formulation of the *New Directions in Creativity* series. Suggestions for the teacher on how to best use the program's activities and enhance its effects are included.
Subject Matter and Teaching Strategy:	Each activity requires a class period to complete, so the program could be used with whole classroom groups in language arts activities. The follow-up suggestions for each activity can be used to extend the material and ideas into other classroom subjects. The program could also be used effectively in an individualized or open classroom.

Rationale: *New Directions in Creativity* has been produced in answer to a recognized need for effective, research-based curricular materials for developing children's creativity. The program is based on evidence that all children have potential for creative thought and that the exercise of their creative abilities will result in cognitive growth.

What:	*People Projects* by Merril Harmin
Published By:	Addison Wesley Publishing Co. Language Arts Group Sand Hill Rd. Menlo Park, California 94025
How To Order:	Order from publisher or contact local Addison-Wesley representative. List price: $27.00 Consummable items: None.
Description:	*People Projects* are imaginative task cards presenting activities for individual students or small groups. The activities are concerned with values, problem solving, action, feelings, and imagination.
Target Audience:	Intermediate grade levels (4–6) and up.
Materials Provided:	There are three sets (A,B, and C). Each set consists of 40 People Project cards. Each card is sturdy and colorfully printed, suitable for individual student use or bulletin board display, and presents one situation for the students to try out.
Teacher's Guide:	A brief Teacher's Manual is included with each packet of *People Projects*. It summarizes the goals and broad purposes of the material, and identifies additional resources and procedures for evaluation.
Subject Matter and Teaching Strategy:	The *People Projects* cut across traditional curriculum areas, and provide opportunities to develop a variety of cognitive and effective processes: listening skills, inquiry, sharing and comparing experiences, self-direction in learning, etc. They are intended to be enjoyable projects which children can do (alone or in groups) and share with others.
Rationale:	The *People Projects* program is designed to help teachers provide enjoyable learning experiences that will integrate complex cognitive processes (such as creative thinking and

problem solving) with affective concerns (self-understanding, self-direction, values clarification, expression, and recognition of feelings etc.).

For Further Reading: Harmin M.; Kirschenbaum, H.; and Simon, S. *Clarifying Values Through Subject Matter.* Minneapolis: Winston Press, 1973.

What:	*Pick-A-Project* Judith Wooster
Published By:	DOK Publishers, Inc. 71 Radcliffe Road Buffalo, New York 14214
How To Order:	Order from publisher List price: $2.00 Consumable items: None
Description:	*Pick-A-Project* is a packet of cards with project ideas on each card designed to provide both teachers and students with motivating and challenging ideas to fit their interests.
Target Audience:	Grades 3–6
Materials Provided:	Forty project idea cards with one to three ideas per card and sample project plan cards are included in the packet. Cards are colorcoded to correspond with the mode of presentation. Green cards describe projects which ask the student to read, research, record and review. Yellow cards contain oral activities involving telling, teaching and talking. Draw, design and display projects are described on red cards. Blue cards deal with activities involving making, modeling, manipulating and moving.
Subject Matter and Teaching Strategy:	*Pick-A-Project* cards may be used in a variety of ways. Teachers may utilize project ideas in planning lessons, units and group activities as well as setting up learning centers. The cards may be used by students to help them carry out individual projects to fit their interests and needs. Card ideas are flexible, and are easily adapted to meet a wide range of subject areas and topics.
Rationale:	Projects should be provided for students which allow for freedom of expression within a vast range of interest areas. Gifted students have varying needs and interests—project idea cards aid students in exploring interest areas while allowing them to select presentation modes that most appeal to individual styles.

What:	*The Productive Thinking Program* Martin V. Covington, Richard S. Crutchfield, Lillian Davies, Robert M. Olton
Published By:	Charles E. Merrill Publishing Company A division of Bell and Howell Company 1300 Alum Creek Drive Columbus, Ohio 43216
How To Order:	Order from publisher. List price: $150.00 Consumable items: Spirit duplicating masters.
Description:	The *Productive Thinking Program* is a suspensefilled learning experience that teaches high-level thinking skills. Students become imaginative detectives and improve their thinking skills by solving mystery cases. Student participation in the program will result in improvement of the following skills: Recognizing puzzling facts. Asking relevant, information-seeking questions. Solving problems in new ways. Generating ideas of high quality. Evaluating ideas. Achieving solutions to problems.
Target Audience:	Grades 5 and 6.
Materials Provided:	A 35″ × 47″ chart of Thinking Guides for classroom display. Fifteen Basic Lesson Booklets in cartoon form. Included in the Basic Lesson Booklets are Problem Sets. These are supplementary materials for further extension and strengthening of skills taught in basic lessons. Teacher's Guide.
Teacher's Guide:	Explains the program, provides administration procedures, discussion of lessons and problem sets, and follow-up activities for the teacher. Spirit Duplicating Masters of 14 special activity sheets accompany the basic lessons.

Subject
Matter
and
Teaching
Strategy:

The *Productive Thinking Program* is an individualized study program for students, with opportunities for group discussion and application of skills learned.

The program fits well into the language arts curriculum with emphasis on reading, writing, analyzing facts, organizing thoughts, and thinking critically. The program can also be integrated into a social studies area. It provides skills in generating ideas, looking at things in new ways, imagining different possibilities, and thinking creatively.

The format of the program adapts well for effective use in learning centers. The exercises also serve as springboards for discussion. Small groups could work as teams and become cooperative case-breakers.

Rationale:

The *Productive Thinking Program* teaches children how to think, not what to think. Direct training of thinking skills to develop students' full potential for solution of problems of any nature can be developed. These are generalized skills, underlying all sorts of problem solving. These productive thinking skills are developed using the context of meaningful problems that motivate the student to use his mind in an independent way.

What:	*The Purdue Creative Thinking Program*
Published By:	Gifted Education Resource Institute Purdue University West Lafayette, Indiana
How To Order:	John F. Feldhusen, Gifted Education Resource Institute, Education Department Purdue University, West Lafayette, Indiana 47907 List price: $125 For: Thirty two taped programs and one set of 3–4 exercises per program. Consumable items: Exercise worksheets.
Description:	*The Purdue Creative Thinking Program* consists of 32 audiotaped programs and a set of three or four printed exercises for each program. The taped program consists of two parts: a three- to four-minute presentation designed to teach a principle or idea for improving creative thinking, and an eight- to ten-minute story about a famous American pioneer. The exercises for each progams consist of printed directions, problems, or questions which are designed to provide practice in originality, flexibility, fluency, and elaboration in thinking.
Target Audience:	Grade levels 4, 5, and 6.
Materials Provided:	Cassette tapes. 32 programs on 8 tapes, each 15 minutes long, giving specific suggestions for creative thinking and an historical story narrated by a professional radio announcer and dramatized with sound effects and background music. The program closes with an introduction to the first creativity exercise.
Exercise worksheets:	A series of three or four creativity exercises accompanies each tape. The exercises are to be duplicated on 8 ½″ × 11″ paper and distributed to students. One set of exercises for each tape is provided with the initial order.
Teacher's Guide:	A teacher's manual accompanies the program. It gives a brief description and rationale of the program. Written transcripts of the audiotapes are presented along with a statement of the required exercises. General guidelines for the teacher are also provided for help in using the series, along with a set of specific directions for proper administration of the program.

Subject
Matter
and
Teaching
Strategy:

The content of the audiotapes focuses on social studies. The series also teaches skills (writing and listening) which are relevant to the language arts.

The program is designed to be administered in a group setting. It can be easily adapted to in individualized learning center activity.

Rationale:

The program is designed to develop student's divergent thinking skills. Specifically, the exercises provide training in fluent, flexible, original, and elaborative thinking. These thinking skills increase a child's creative thinking and problem-solving ability.

What:	*Secrets and Surprises* Joe Wayman and Lorraine Plum
Published By:	Good Apple, Inc. Box 229 Carthage, Illinois 62321
How To Order:	Order from publisher List price: $7.95 Consumable items: None
Description:	*Secrets and Surprises* consists of eighteen units each divided into three parts: Motivation, Move and Imagine, and Related Activities. The units are designed to develop language skills, imagination, concentration, sensory awareness, self-concept, social interaction, spontaneity and psychomotor skills.
Target Audience:	Grades K–8
Materials Provided:	One *Secrets and Surprises* book
Subject Matter and Teaching Strategy:	Each unit begins with a motivation goal, a short activity or reading which the teacher presents to the class. This is followed by a move and imagine activity aimed at building creative thinking skills, psychomotor abilities, self-concept, and sensitivity to oneself, others and the use of space. Each unit concludes with several related activities, including brainstorming and individual and group projects, which aid writing, speaking, listening, creativity and other skills.
Rationale:	Children's energy can be used to facilitate learning if the teacher incorporates movement and imagination into the regular classroom learning. Language development should include not only intellectual processes, but also emotional and physical aspects of development. This book provides the structure and stimuli for children to create their own experiences, thus developing language not from words, but from images and experiences.

What:	*Social Studies Activities for the Gifted Student* Barbara Ann Martin
Published By:	DOK Publishers, Inc. 71 Radcliffe Raod Buffalo, New York 14214
How To Order:	Order from publisher List price: $2.50 Consumable items: None
Description:	This book presents intriguing social studies enrichment activities especially geared to stimulate the high level thinking powers of the gifted. Chapters deal with U.S. History, Government and current events, and the Future versus the Past. Activities include tracing family trees, researching old cemeteries, preparing documentaries, and planning communities.
Target Audience:	Grades 4–8
Materials Provided:	One activity book
Sujbect Matter and Teaching Strategy:	Activities are social studies oriented, and are intended to foster independent study and self-direction. Activities originally require some teacher direction, but students gradually become more responsible for their own learning through researching and organizing information. Additional activities are suggested, but it is hoped students will form their own ideas and individual learning experiences.
Rationale:	Because gifted children are a vital natural resource, social studies is an important area to develop. With the problems facing our world today, gifted individuals hold the key to future solutions. *Social Studies Activities for the Gifted* is intended to develop self-instruction skills while introducing children to social studies topics in the hopes that students will be better able to recognize and solve future dilemmas.

What:	*The Spice Series* Educational Service, Inc.
Published By:	Educational Service, Inc. P.O. Box 219 Stevensville, Michigan 49127
How To Order:	Order from publisher or school supply dealer. List price: $5.25 each for Handbooks. Consumable items: Duplicating masters. $3.95 each.
Description:	*The Spice Series* consists of 26 handbooks of ideas particularly chosen to aid the teacher in motivating student interest in classroom subjects. Each handbook contains directions for preparation, lists of materials needed, and instructions for students for class activities, games, projects, and experiments. Many art and creative writing ideas are presented in the series. There are also 33 sets of duplicating masters.
Target Audience:	Kindergarten—grade 8.
Materials Provided:	Each title in the *Spice Series* is an individual handbook which may be purchased separately from the others. A partial list of materials follows:

Spice: A handbook of language arts teaching ideas to be used with kindergarten through fourth grades. The activities, games, and lessons suggested in the book are designed to add interest and motivation to the regular language arts program.

Spice Series Duplicating Masters.
> Volume 1: grades kindergarten through two.
> Volume 2: grades two through four.

Probe: A handbook of ideas for teaching elementary science. The lesson ideas were chosen to stimulate children to find question-provoking aspects of their environment and search for answers. The handbook emphasizes activity and discovery methods of teaching and learning. Ideas are included to help teachers promote scientific speculation, to help them set up simple experiments, and to help them teach simple concepts by the inquiry method.

Plus: A handbook of ideas for motivating interest in elementary mathematics.

Spark: A handbook of ideas for motivating interest in elementary social studies.

Create: A handbook of ideas for art activities. Using easily found materials, the art activities allow students opportunities to be truly creative with new ideas and to approach old ideas and material from a new perspective. Many ideas can be adapted for use with language arts, social studies, and science projects.

Action: A handbook of ideas for motivating interest in elementary physical education.

Stage: A handbook of ideas which allow students to be creative in dramatic activities. Suggestions are included for choral readings, class plays, pantomime, role-playing, and impromptu skits. Many ideas do not require staging or special materials. Instructions are included to aid teachers in producing more elaborate stage productions requiring scenery, properties, costumes, lights, and sound effects.

Rescue: A handbook of ideas for promoting the interest of remedial students in reading.

Anchor: A handbook of ideas for motivating interest in language arts in grades four through eight.

Pride: A handbook of black studies techniques which helps black students develop positive self-concepts, and pride, and knowledge of black history, African geography, African animals, and famous black people.

Launch: A handbook of ideas to motivate interest in learning for teachers of preschool and kindergarten children.

Press: A handbook of teaching ideas to motivate learning through the use of the newspaper.

Flair: A handbook of ideas for teachers to use in motivating student interest in creative writing. Writing activities which capture student interest are suggested. Creative writing and poetry forms such as haiku, syo, and diamontes are illustrated.

Teacher's Guide: Each idea entry in each handbook contains specific directions for carrying out that activity.

Subject Matter and Teaching Strategy: The *Spice Series* consists of 26 handbooks and 33 sets of duplicating masters which cover topics in the elementary school curriculum. Many ideas can be adapted to serve several purposes. Activities in one subject can be designed to correlate with studies in another subject. Teachers will find ideas for enrichment, remediation, total class projects, small group activities, and individual seatwork. Many can be adapted to fit a learning center or a self-instructional format.

Rationale: The *Spice Series* is a group of teacher handbooks which provide teachers with suggested activities for creative thinking and practical ideas for making learning fun and interesting for children. They are written from the point-of-view that children are interested in what is happening in the here and now and not in learning to be prepared for the future.

What:	*Story Starters—Intermediate Level* *Primary Level*
Published By:	Creative Teaching Press, Inc. 5305 Production Drive Huntington Beach, California 92649
How To Order:	Order from publisher. List price: $4.95. Consumable items: None.
Description:	*Story Starters* brings together 50 illustrated ideas that interest and motivate students to express themselves creatively. Each Story Starter card presents an interesting situation that the child can write about and extend. The subjects that are dealt with are those that are most stimulating and relevant to the experiences and imagination of young children. Many involve adventure and fantasy and require good use of the imagination. Some of the subjects involved are buried treasure, castles, sports, and animals.
Target Audience:	Set 1: Intermediate elementary. Set 2: Primary
Materials Provided:	Fifty 5″ × 8″ cards of story starters, accompanying illustrations, and word lists. Teacher's Guide. Suggestions to the student.
Teacher's Guide:	Each kit includes suggestions for the teacher on how to use *Story Starters*. The suggestions describe various setups for individual and group use.
Subject Matter and Teaching Strategy:	*Story Starters* may be used with an entire class working on one idea at a time. For more individualized situations, a writing center is suggested where students may choose a card and work on it. Children may also illustrate their stories and present them to the class as a project. For a project, students can dramatize their stories individually or in groups for presentation to other classes, parents, or the teacher.

144

Rationale: *Story Starters* uses a variety of writing experiences to develop children's creative thinking abilities. Children are motivated by using relevant, interesting, and exciting subject matter. The combination of illustrations, ideas, and suggested words provides the motivating force for unlocking their individuality and developing skills.

What:	*Sunflowering* Bob Stanish
Published By:	Good Apple, Inc. Box 299 Cathage, Illinois 62321
How To Order:	Order from publisher List price: $7.95 Consumable items: None
Description:	*Sunflowering* activities deal with four basic conditions to encourage imagination development, creative expression and sensitivity: imagery analogy strategies, object-to-object analogy strategies, person-to-object analogy strategies, and transforming strategies. The book describes unusual activities which combine cognitive and affective development tasks, following the author's premise that "knowledge, if it's going to be effectively learned and applied, has to be integrated into who we are, and into how we view and live life." (p. 6).
Target Audience:	Grades 1–8.
Materials Provided:	One *Sunflowering* book.
Teacher's Guide:	A thorough introduction explains the author's purpose as well as suggesting strategies for use of the book.
Subject Matter and Teaching Strategy:	No specific subject matter is stressed. *Sunflowering* provides higher thinking experiences, seeing imagination and creative expression as processes of absorbing and applying knowledge. Sensitivity development is also encouraged because this area has such tremendous influence on other cognitive processes. *Sunflowering* techniques are designed to go beyond traditional learning of information and to facilitate application of thinking processes.

Teachers are asked to accept all student responses in order to promote imagination and creative expression in an accepting atmosphere. Questions posed should be open-ended, and the teacher should pause frequently after questions or in discussions to allow students time for visualizing and feeling. Grading is strongly discouraged.

146

The book contains no chapters and teachers may follow activities through from start to finish or skip around, using the "strategy mapping chart" for optimal distribution of activities.

Rationale: *Sunflowering* looks at everything in the universe as being interrelated. Life is viewed as a metaphor, and the discovery of unique and interesting associations between images, objects and persons is therefore basic to the development of imagination, creativity and sensitivity. The growth of these thinking and feeling processes is of the utmost importance for today's students to meet future needs in an intelligent, sensitive, and human fashion.

What:	*Tales of Giants*
	Joyce Kohfeldt
Published By:	Prentice Hall Learning Systems, Inc.
	P.O. Box 47X
	Englewood Cliffs, New Jersey 07632
How To Order:	Order from publisher
	List price: $5.50
	Consumable items: None
Description:	These units attempt to provide interesting and imaginative materials for teaching creative writing, proofreading, editing, and reference skills.
Target Audience:	Grades 4–7.
Materials Provided:	Each of the units in the 62 page book focuses on some aspect of the theme "giants." There are five units, including an extended set of materials concerning a "travel agency." There is also a classroom wall chart to use in conjunction with the units.
Teacher's Guide:	Each unit includes a brief description of suggested teaching ideas and teacher preparation.
Subject Matter and Teaching Strategy:	The focus of the units is on language, writing, and reference skills. They could be used in a variety of ways with the whole class, with small groups, and as individualized instruction units.
Rationale:	The author attempts to use giants and legendary characters as a focus for integrating several different types of learning activities.

What:	*Think-Ins* Sandra Nina Kaplan Sheila Kunishima Madsen
Published By:	Creative Teaching Press, Inc. 5305 Production Drive Huntington Beach, California 92649
How To Order:	Order from publisher. List price: $6.95. Consumable items: None.
Description:	*Think-Ins* is a series of 30 task cards that provide ideas and suggestions to stimulate creative thinking and problem solving. Each card is on a different topic that concerns mankind and his environment, and presents a challenge, things to think about, suggestions for activities, plus ideas for further inquiry. Sample topics are propaganda, education, overpopulation, garbage, and health. The problems that are presented in the challenge are to be solved through the processes described in the sections that follow. Hypothesizing, researching, discovering facts, and drawing conclusions are some of the processes that the student practices and should learn from the program.
Target Audience:	Grades 4–12.
Materials Provided:	Thirty task cards made of heavy paper, with the challenge and other sections, and an accompanying photograph.
Teacher's Guide:	An introduction to the teacher is presented that explains the format and rationale of the set.
Subject Matter and Teaching Strategy:	Each activity is directed towards the individual student. The series can be used in a learning center, for independent study and as enrichment activities. The *further research* section suggests ideas for more in-depth research that could be useful as projects and long-term assignments.
Rationale:	*Think-Ins* is based on the concept that students should become involved in topical problems, situations, and ideas, and should actively generate their own hypotheses and solutions pertaining to those problems. This process is designed to encourage and develop problem-solving skills and facilitate individual expression.

What:	*Thinklab* and *Thinklab 2*
	K.J. Weber
Published By:	Science Research Associates (Canada) Ltd.
	Toronto, Canada
How To Order:	Order from publisher
	Science Research Associates
	Order Services Department
	155 N. Wacker Drive
	Chicago, Illinois 60606
	List price: Thinklab $88; Thinklab 2 $118.67
	Consumable items: None
Description:	*Thinklab* kits have been developed to stimulate cognitive development, especially insight, reflection, and creativity. The kits are also designed to be motivating reading programs. Cards are arranged according to type of cognitive problem and difficulty level, and are especially helpful in motivating the bright academic student to think about creative and logical problem-solving activities.
Target Audience:	Grade 3—Adult (*Thinklab*)
	Grade 5—Adult (*Thinklab 2*)
Materials Provided:	*Thinklabs* are stored in sturdy and colorful plastic boxes. Thinklab includes 500 cards (4 copies of 125 different cards) and Thinklab 2 contains 700 cards (4 copies of 145 cards and 8 copies of 15 cards). Kits also come with manipulative materials, student progress cards, and a Teacher's Guide. Cards are color-coded for easy identification of type of problem.
Teacher's Guide:	Elaborate information is given concerning the program, its purposes and its objectives. Research evidence is cited which supports the effectiveness of the program. Possible solutions to the problems are also given in the guide.
Subject Matter and Teaching Strategy:	*Thinklab* includes five basic types of problems: object manipulation, perception, creative insight, perceiving image patterns, and logical analysis. *Thinklab 2* contains six different kinds of problems. Object manipulation, creative insight, logical analysis, quantitative thinking, brainstorming, and just for fun. Abilities challenged come from the middle and upper levels of Bloom's taxonomy,

150

and problems are framed in non-academic terms to retain high motivation.

It is suggested that students begin with the lower numbered problems and work through consecutively, although it is possible to skip around according to type of problem. Students record their own achievement on student progress cards.

Because many of the problems require creative thinking, it is important for the teacher to accept more than one correct answer.

Rationale: This program is challenging for any student in the areas of creative and logical problem solving. Although it is beneficial for the unmotivated student, it is also extremely stimulating and challenging to the gifted student, because of the wide variety of difficulty levels included. An important use is with the gifted child who is bored or apathetic, as the problems are motivating and extend beyond common curricular areas.

What:	*A Total Creativity Program for Individualizing and Humanizing the Learning Process* Frank E. Williams
Published By:	Educational Technology Publications 140 Sylvan Avenue Englewood Cliffs, New Jersey 07632
How To Order:	Order from publisher. List price: $79.95 Consumable items: None.
Description:	The *Total Creativity Program* is designed to give teachers the practical help they have been seeking in identifying, encouraging, and assessing children's creative talents in the classroom. It provides classroom teachers, curriculum supervisors, and building principals with assessment and identification measures, teaching strategies, resource listings, lesson plans, posters, and demonstration lesson audiotape cassettes in the area of creativity. Many examples of applied activities for creative thinking and feeling in the elementary school program are offered. A number of activities are suggested for teachers to use in modifying or elaborating on the *Total Creativity Program* in order to meet their own individual classroom needs.
Target Audience:	Kindergarten through upper elementary grades.
Materials Provided:	The *Total Creativity Program* consists of eleven components which are packaged in a vinyl carrying case: *Volume 1—Identifying and Measuring Creative Potential.* This book presents various observational and assessment measures for the classroom teacher to aid in identifying and measuring the thinking and feeling processes which contribute to creativity. *Volume 2—Encouraging Creativity Potential.* This book offers a repertoire of activities and strategies which can be used to encourage each child's creative potential. *Volume 3—Teacher's Workbook.* This workbook provides teachers and teacher trainers with supplementary instruments, checklists and worksheet exercises for observing and assessing teacher and pupil creative behavior. The checklists and worksheets may be detached and reproduced.

152

Volume 4—Media Resource Book. This book offers an extensive listing and classification of books, films, and currently available curriculum materials to teach creative thinking and feeling.

Volume 5—Classroom Ideas for Encouraging Thinking and Feeling. This book offers over 380 lesson-plan ideas to stimulate creative thinking in a variety of subject areas (i.e., language arts, social studies, science, arithmetic, art-music). The suggested lessons call for processes of inquiry, discovery, and creative problem solving.

Poster Set 1—Thinking-Feeling Processes. This set of eight black-and-white posters depicts each of the thinking-feeling processes stressed in the *Program.*

Poster Set 2—Teaching Strategies. This set of nineteen black-and-white posters depicts each teaching strategy recommended for use in the program. One poster in this set gives an overview of the conceptual model used in the *Program.*

Teaching Strategies Packet. This packet of nineteen cards describes specific examples of a strategy that can be used to inspire the creative thinking and feeling of pupils in five subject areas of a curriculum.

Teacher Training Audiotape Cassettes. One cassette, entilted "Creativity: A Bridge Between Thinking and Feeling," presents information on the rationale for the teaching of creative thinking and feeling. A second cassette, entitled "Demonstration Lesson," presents actual classroom sessions in which the principles of this program were originally field-tested.

Teacher's Guide:

The *Instructor's Manual* explains the use and rationale of the materials in the kit, offers a suggested sequence for applying the program and using the kit, and contains instructions for using the demonstration lesson cassette. Transcripts of the "demonstration lesson cassette" are included.

Subject Matter and Teaching Strategy:

The *Total Creativity Program* may be used on a daily basis throughout the school year within the existing curriculum. The teacher is encouraged to select activities or materials from the program to meet specific class needs or interests. The activities and strategies which are offered

153

can be applied to regular classroom practices to encourage thinking and feeling in pupils as they learn regular subject matter (i.e., language arts, science, arithmetic, social studies, art-music).

Rationale: The *Total Creativity Program* has been designed around a conceptual model which emphasizes teaching creativity through subject matter content. This model emphasizes four intellective behaviors and four feeling behaviors appropriate to productive-divergent thinking: fluent thinking, flexible thinking, original thinking, elaborative thinking and curiosity, risk-taking, complexity, and imagination.

The *Program* is based upon the rationale that there are mental abilities and emotional capacities of children that are untapped by traditional teaching methods, that these untapped abilities and capacities can be systematically utilized while simultaneously learning subject matter content, and that the most effective means for doing this is through the use of multiple teaching strategies.

What:	*Wonderwork* Margaret S. Woods
Published By:	DOK Publishers, Inc. 71 Radcliffe Road Buffalo, New York 14214
How To Order:	Order from publisher. List price: $2.25. Consumable items: None.
Description:	*Wonderwork* presents a series of experiences for the elementary school child designed to arouse curiosity and encourage the child's spontaneous expression through dramatic play, creative art and creative dramatics. It is a guide for teachers who work with children in nursery school, kindergarten, libraries, and the home. It suggests how to release a child's unique potential through learning experiences initiated by teacher and learner. With the aid of various audiovisual materials (i.e., recordings, poems, storybooks) the teacher arouses the curiosity of the children about a particular aspect of the world around them. Questions are also used to open children's interest and imagination to a variety of things such as caterpillars, leaves, Jack Frost, spiders, and so on. A poem is presented to develop a picture of the theme being discussed. The themes are generally oriented to the four seasons of the year. Spontaneous expression with feeling and movement is encouraged by the use of various "let's pretend" exercises in which the children become the thing being talked about (e.g., a spider, a jack-in-the-box, a leaf, etc.) and, with the aid of music, dance and play, move just as these things would move. Each child communicates his/her own unique ideas and feelings to peers. Inquiry and discovery are fostered through supplementary activities in which each child explores other dimensions of the topic being discussed.
Target Audience:	Nursery school and kindergarten.
Materials Provided:	One *Wonderwork* booklet.

Teacher's Guide:	The *Wonderwork* booklet is a guide for teachers and parents which provides interesting suggestions on how to develop the capacity for wonder in the young child. Many recordings, poems, and picture books could be used with the *Wonderwork* booklet. Teachers are encouraged to make their own choice.
Subject Matter and Teaching Strategy:	*Wonderwork* guides are planned for use in the various seasons of the year. Each unit deals with appropriate events and objects that occur during these seasons. The first series of *Wonderwork* guides, for example, are planned for use in the fall and early winter seasons. The subject matter for this series deals with hinges, leaves, maple wings, caterpillars, spiders, dandelion plants, Halloween, a bottle floating in the sea, Jack Frost, Thanksgiving, Jack-in-the-box, and Christmas trees. Various learning objectives for each lesson are given, each objective designed to enhance the awareness, sensitivity, and appreciation of the things discussed in the lesson.
	Curiosity can be aroused when the children are asked to describe their experiences or wonder at the things under consideration (e.g., "Have any of you ever seen Jack Frost?", "Who knows the caterpillar's secret?"). Expression is encouraged by "let's pretend" exercises. This expression, sensitively recognized by the teacher, becomes a joyful source of communication for the children.
Rationale:	*Wonderwork* is based upon the rationale that a child can learn many valuable things if his/her curiosity is aroused and if productive learning experiences are provided. The experiences require channels for expression to guide and facilitate the flow of feelings which accompany the learning experience. These channels are optimally open through dramatic play, creative art, and rhythmic movement. Such meaningful learning experiences provide a wealth of materials for further activities in learning.
For Further Reading:	Torrance, E.P. *Encouraging Creativity in the Classroom.* Dubuque, Iowa: William C. Brown Company Publishers, 1970.

Williams, F. *Classroom Ideas for Encouraging Thinking and Feeling*. Buffalo, New York: DOK Publishers, Inc., 1970.

Woods, M.S., and Trithart, B. *Guidelines to Creative Dramatics*. Buffalo, New York: DOK Publishers, Inc., 1970.

What:	*The Writing Center.*
Published By:	Winston Press 430 Oak Grove, Suite 203 Minneaplis, Minnesota 55403
How To Order:	Order from publisher. School price: $29.95 Consumable items: Lined writing paper.
Description:	*The Writing Center* is designed to stimulate children's imaginations and provide encouragement for creative writing. The ideas presented in the kit spark imagination and help children develop their writing skills.
Target Audience:	Grades 3 through 8.
Materials Provided:	The *Center* includes 49 "Idea Generators," each a thick cardboard sheet (8 ¼" × 10 ¼") with a color illustration or photograph and suggestions for writing about the ideas, objects, or events. The Ideas are categorized into five (5) areas: adventure, mystery, fantasy, animals, and poetry. Lined paper is also included.
Teacher's Guide:	A list of objectives with suggestions for their use and evaluation is included.
Subject Matter and Teaching Strategy:	Each "Idea Generator" can serve as a basis for individual writing and discussion. Children can write their own stories and ideas or participate in group discussion of the illustrations. *The Writing Center* may be used to its fullest advantage as a weekly activity.
Rationale:	*The Writing Center* uses imaginative activities as the basis for developing creative thinking. Through the encouragement and practice in creative writing that is provided by *The Writing Center,* the child gains experience and confidence in creative production.

SOME RECOMMENDED BOOKS ON GIFTED EDUCATION AND ON TEACHING CREATIVE THINKING AND PROBLEM SOLVING

CREATIVE LEARNING AND TEACHING

E. Paul Torrance and R. E. Myers
1970
List price: $10.95
How to order: Harper & Row, Publishers
10 East 53rd Street
New York, New York 10022

This is an exciting book about teaching creative thinking. Its message is not limited to any particular educational level nor to any particular group of people. It is especially useful to teachers, but it can be used by administrators, supervisors, curriculum specialists, and interested laymen. The book attempts to aid teachers by increasing their awareness of their own creative potentialities and by improving their skills in identifying, developing, and cultivating the creative abilities of their students.

While theoretical considerations are not neglected, the book is primarily concerned with the things the teacher can do in the classroom to foster creativity. Some examples of what the book offers to the teacher include ways in which the teacher can acquire skills to facilitate creative learning and ways in which the teacher can understand children. Chapters are also included which are concerned with improving the teacher's ability to ask questions, foster a more creative environment, and be more creative. The book also contains sample problems and illustrations of how the material could be used in the classroom.

The authors' personal styles of writing make the book easy to read and easy to use as a source in improving teachers' and students' creative abilities.

CREATIVE SCIENCING I AND II

Alfred DeVito and Gerald H. Krockover
1976
List price: *Creative Sciencing I,* A Practical Approach, $7.95
    Creative Sciencing II, Ideas and Activities for Teachers and Children, $7.95
How to order: Little Brown and Company
    34 Beacon street
    Boston, Massachusetts 02106

Creative Sciencing I: A Practical Approach sets forth guidelines and specific suggestions of things teachers can do to incorporate a "creative-sciencing approach into their present teaching style and attitudes. It details how to employ such useful strategies as interest centers, task cards, modules, and individualization . . . how to introduce "creative-sciencing methods and techniques into virtually every subject skill or concept you present or reinforce . . . no matter whether you teach primary, intermediate, or middle school children. "Creative sciencing" as promoted in this text is more than just good science: it is good reading, language arts, social studies, mathematics, art, music, and health and physical education. It is the integration of all areas of the curriculum with the attitudes, ideals, and spirit of science.

Creative Sciencing II: Ideas and Activities for Teachers and Children is divided into three parts, Part I, "Brainstorming in Science" presents over 100 classroom activities. The activities were selected for their creativeness, student-teacher involvement, and potential content. They require little background in science, and they do not call for special or expensive equipment and supplies. Each activity is designed to present teachers with an idea, which is then expanded into a creative sciencing endeavor. Part II, "Shoestring Sciencing" is included as a reaction to the cost of science equipment and as a proof of the idea that sciencing takes more thinking and decision making than it does equipment. Part III, "Science Skills and Techniques" acquaints teachers with an explanation of the skills and techniques needed for creative sciencing.

CREATIVE TEACHING GAMES

Linda Polon and Wendy Pollitt
1974
List price: $6.95
How to order: T.S. Denison and Company, Inc.
         9601 Newton Avenue S.
         Minneapolis, Minnesota 55431
         (Order No. SBN—513–01265–6)

Creative Teaching Games describes over forty educational games that are designed to stimulate and motivate children to learn in enjoyable ways. The games can be used with almost every subject taught in the elementary grades. Many of the games deal with reading. Other games cover primary math concepts. The games may be played by one person at a time or in groups of two or three. Most of the games are competitive.

Each game is described in detail. The teacher is informed of how many children can play and what each child is to do during the game. The educational purpose of the game is described in terms of the reading or math skills that are used during the game. The teacher is told what materials are needed for the game and suggestions are made on how to make the game boards more durable for repeated use. Drawings accompany the text so as to make the construction of each game easily understandable.

This book is a highly readable guide to educational games which can be used in the elementary classroom. The games are readily modifiable to a wide range of subject matter taught in the elementary grades.

THE CREATIVELY GIFTED CHILD

Suggestions for Parents and Teachers
Joe Khatena
1978
List price: $6.95 (plus $1.35 postage and handling)
How to order: Allan Associates, Inc.
         P.O. Drawer B
         Starkville, Mississippi 39759

This book emphasizes the importance of parents and teachers in recognizing and identifying creatively gifted children through testing, and then in encouraging them to develop their intellectual potential.

Dr Khatena sees teachers and parents as catalysts for the creatively gifted child to interact in the world. The book outlines the methods of testing to identify these special children; I.Q. tests, creative thinking ability tests, and the like, which identify both strengths and weaknesses of the gifted child. Then the author includes exercises to encourage the child in creative thinking and problem solving. He also gives several suggestions to both teachers and parents to help support the child, reward her, reduce her anxieties, encourage her to approach learning as experimentation, so that the child becomes enthusiastic about developing her creative characteristics and making a contribution to the community in which she lives.

The book is of great value to all those who are interested in the special problems of creatively gifted children. Dr. Khatena offers sensitive insight into dealing with these children and enabling them to fully use their potential.

DEVELOPING CREATIVITY IN THE GIFTED AND TALENTED

Carolyn M. Callahan
1979
List price: $4.50
How to order: The Council for Exceptional Children
                 1920 Association Drive
                 Reston, Virginia 22091

Developing Creativity in the Gifted and Talented is an excellent introduction to research and instructional materials for teaching creativity to gifted children. The book was especially designed to organize and clarify for the teacher of the gifted the vast amount of material now available on creativity training.

Four major sections comprise *Developing Creativity in the Gifted and Talented*:

Chapter one presents various definitions and models of creativity. Chapter two describes several measures to assess creativity. The third chapter is the major focus of the book, containing important concepts and research findings as well as references for the reader who wishes to pursue the topic in depth. Teacher guides are provided in this chapter to exemplify techniques described. The final section suggests methods of evaluating a program's effectiveness.

EDUCATING THE ABLEST

John C. Gowan, Joe Khatena, & E. Paul Torrance (Eds.)
1979
List price: $10.95
How to order: F.E. Peacock Publishers
                 401 West Irving Park Road
                 Itasca, Illinois
                 60143

This is a collection of articles from the pages of the Gifted *Child Quarterly* edited by three eminent leaders in gifted education and creativity. All the major leaders in gifted education and creativity, from J.P. Guilford to Julian C. Stanley are represented. The major topics around which the articles are organized include

1. introduction and history
2. developmental characteristics
3. programs
4. curricula
5. guidances
6. identification and evaluation
7. teachers and teachers training
8. parents
9. creativity
10. disadvantaged gifted youth
11. women
12. imagery and hemisphericity

There is also a concluding section which looks to the future with readings by John C. Gowan, Stanley Krippner, E. Paul Torrance and others. This book represents a major resource reference for gifted education. It should be in all school professional libraries for teachers. It provides an abundance of guidance and direction for developers of programs and curricula in gifted education.

THE ENRICHMENT TRIAD MODEL

Joseph S. Renzulli
1977
List price: $7.95
How to order: Creative Learning Press
              P.O. Box 320
              Mansfield Center, Connecticut
              06250

This is a guide for school personnel who are attempting to develop enrichment programs for gifted students, especially at the elementary and junior high levels. The Triad model is well known among gifted educators and has been used as a model for gifted programs in many schools. The model posits three kinds of instructional activity for the gifted:

1. general exploratory
2. group training
3. individual and small group investigations of real problems

The Triad activities are developed in close relationship with the regular school curriculum. The Appendix offers the famous "Interest-A-Lyzer" which is used to assess student interests, skills and experiential backgrounds as a prelude and guide for independent project activity. It also includes the "Community Talent Miner," an instrument used to assess potential community contributors to a gifted program.

THE GIFTED STUDENT: AN ANNOTATED BIBLIOGRAPHY

Jean Laubenfels
1977
List price: $15.00
How to order: Greenwood Press, Inc.
              51 Riverside Avenue
              Westport, Connecticut
              06880

This book covers the field of giftedness and gifted education. Most of the annotations provide sufficient information about the source to make it possible to evaluate the value of the information. The annotations cover the following: (1) the history of gifted education, (2) causal factors and characteristics,

(3) identification, (4) programs, (5) longitudinal studies, (6) creative research, (7) special problems of the gifted, and (8) instruments or tests useful in identifying the gifted. Under programs the annotations cover all basic curricular areas, administration, and counselling and guidance. It is clear that the field of gifted education lacks high quality research but is characterized by many program development projects. This book is a must for researchers and program developers who wish to assess the current state of knowledge in gifted education.

THE GIFTED AND THE TALENTED: THEIR EDUCATION AND DEVELOPMENT

A. Harry Passow (Editor)
1979
List price: $14.00
How to order: University of Chicago Press
5801 Ellis Avenue
Chicago, Illinois
60637

This is the Seventy-Eighth Yearbook of the National Society for The Study of Education, Part 1. It presents a comprehensive coverage of topics in the field of gifted education by a host of current leaders and practitioners in the field. Abraham J. Tannenbaum sets the stage with an historical introduction and James J. Gallagher discusses issues in education of the gifted. State and national concerns are discussed by David M. Jackson and Jeffrey Zettel. Programming approaches are discussed by Lynn Fox. There is an excellent chapter on preschool gifted children by Holbert B. Robinson and others. Social studies and language arts in the elementary school are discussed by Sandra N. Kaplan while Daniel P. Keating discusses secondary programs. Other specialized chapters deal with college programs (by Milton J. Gold), community based programs (by June Cox), career education (by Bruce G. Milne) and parent involvment (by Carol N. Nathan). There are still many other chapters (27 in all) dealing with diverse but important issues in gifted education. This book is a major source book for this field.

GROWING UP GIFTED

Barbara Clark
1979
List price: $16.95
How to order: Charles E. Merril Publishing Co.
1300 Alum Creek Drive
Columbus, Ohio 43216

This is a basic text on the nature of giftedness and gifted education. Amply illustrated with photographs, it is a highly readable book which should be of great value to parents, teachers, psychologists and others who are interested in the gifted but are not enrolled in courses of instruction. The book is unique in its offering of a developmental sequence for the growth of the gifted child from birth through adolescence. There is also a strong focus on the teacher (or parent as teacher) and problems of teaching the gifted child. Creativity as it relates to enrichment teaching for the gifted is presented in great depth. The book concludes with a rich set of appendix resources including a section on teaching reading to the preschool gifted, a list of standardized tests used with gifted students, case study forms, and intellectually stimulating games. Overall the book is loaded with valuable information about giftedness and gifted education.

GUIDE TO CREATIVE ACTION

Sidney J. Parnes, Ruth B. Noller, Angelo M. Biondi
1977
List price: $9.95
How to order: Charles Scribner's Sons
597 5th Avenue
New York, New York 10017

A revised and greatly expanded edition of the *Creative Behavior Guidebook*, the new *Guide* is a reference source and teaching manual for the development of creative behavior. Teachers at all grade levels will find this book useful.

The new edition is divided into three parts. The first is concerned with the philosophy and psychology of creative behavior. The second part presents an instructional program for cultivating creative behavior. The program consists of 15 units, each divided into sessions, giving detailed course plans for teaching creative behavior. Part three is entirely new and consists of key readings on cultivating creative behavior. The expanded appendix includes a list of methods and programs for stimulating creativity, a comprehensive bibliography, a list of films on creativity, testing instruments, problems and exercises, and questions and topics for research. In addition, revised outlines of course sections from the first edition are included. The *Creative Action Book* is a revised edition of the original workbook, designed for adult level students.

The *Guide to Creative Action* can be used by teachers at all grade levels, and its basic principles adapted for any classroom. The book is easy to read and well written.

NEW VOICES IN COUNSELING THE GIFTED

Nicholas Colangelo and Ronald Zaffrann
1979
List price: $14.95
How to order: Kendall/Hunt Publishers
                2460 Kerper Boulevard
                Dubuque, Iowa 52001

New Voices in Counseling the Gifted is the first comprehensive treatment of specific issues related to counseling with gifted youngsters. The material includes theoretical approaches to counseling with gifted as well as special issues such as counseling gifted women, culturally diverse gifted, and parents of gifted. The book contains original material reflecting the most current thinking and research in the area by both leading experts and new educators. The book has been espeially designed as a comprehensive text for use in graduate and undergraduate courses on gifted. There is a balance of theoretical, research and practical application articles designed specifically for parents and other interested non-professional educators.

167

PSYCHOLOGY AND EDUCATION OF THE GIFTED

Walter B. Barbe
Josept S. Renzulli
1975
List price: $19.75
How to order: Irvington Publishers
                551 Fifth Avenue
                New York New York
                10017

This is an excellent collection of readings on gifted education. The editors are well known leaders in the field. Most of the major specialists in gifted education authored one or more of the readings. Especially strong are the sections on "Characteristics of the Gifted and Creative" and "Identification and Measurement of Giftedness." The readings on "Developing and Encouraging Giftedness" provide introductions to some excellent resources, but they do not attempt to deal with the areas of the school curriculum and teaching the gifted in those areas. There are some excellent readings on motivating the gifted, on methods of teaching, and the role of the teacher. This book offers a variety of foci on research and application as well as historical and philosophical issues in gifted education. It provides excellent background information for those who will be responsible for program development in gifted education.

PSYCHOLOGY OF PROBLEM-SOLVING THEORY & PRACTICE

Gary R. Davis
1973
List price: $7.95
How to order: Basic Books, Inc., Publishers
                10 East 53rd Street
                New York, New York 10020

The stimulation of creative thinking is a widely accepted goal of education but one that is not ordinarily thought of in terms of observable attainments. This exciting book clarifies the nature of creative human problem-solving skills and describes reasonable principles for their improvement. Attitudes which promote new ideas are explored, cognitive abilities which contribute to the production of new ideas are identified, and particular techniques which help in the generation of ideas are described. Bionics (the biological-based engineering strategy), idea checklists, metaphorical synectics, attribute listing, and brainstorming are just some of the practical techniques that can be effectively used by the elementary teacher.

Psychology of Problem Solving demonstrates how to develop workable and creative solutions to problems. Well researched creative-thinking and problem-solving programs such as the *Saturday Subway Ride, Thinking Creatively,* and *Write? Right!* are thoroughly described. Information on tests and measures of creativity is provided. Teachers will find this clearly written book a good source of ideas for the systematic teaching of problem solving and creativity.

REACH EACH YOU TEACH
A HANDBOOK FOR TEACHERS

Donald J. Treffinger, Robert L. Hohn, & John F. Feldhusen
1979
List price: $3.95
How to order: DOK Publishers
              71 Radcliffe Road
              Buffalo, New York
              14214

This book offers practical assistance to the teacher in planning individualized learning in easy to follow, step-by-step procedures. There are many illustrations and much sample material. Teaching strategies are presented for a variety of thinking processes, and teachers are shown how to set up a record keeping system for the classroom. All of the ideas presented in this book have been field tested by teachers. The book should also be of great value to curriculum planners, teacher trainers, professionals who prepare IEPs and teachers who work with gifted, creative, and talented students. A planning matrix is presented which shows the teacher how to relate specific subject matter content to different levels of thinking processes.

SCAMPER

Robert F. Eberle
1971
List price: $2.50
How to order: DOK Publishers, inc.
           71 Radcliffe Road
           Buffalo, New York 14214

Scamper is a booklet which presents games for the development of imagination in elementary school children.

In the introduction, the author explains the theory and rationale and gives directions for "Scampering." A single child, or a group of children, and one adult can play the *Scamper* games. The teacher presents ideas and cues verbally, and the children are free to explore their own imaginations. The games are designed to increase children's imagination skills, not to develop their skills in a specific subject area.

The theory and directions in the booklet are clearly written and easy to understand. Teachers who wish to increase imaginative abilities and creative skills in their students will find these games helpful.

STIMULATING CREATIVITY

Morris I. Stein
Volume 1, 1974
Volume 2, 1975
List price: $16.50 each volume
How to order: Academic Press
           111 Fifth Avenue
           New York, New York
           10003

These two volumes constitute a major review of research development and theory concerning creativity and problem solving. Volume 1 is subtitled "Individual Procedures" while Volume 2 is subtitled "Group Procedures." In Volume 1 the author discusses the creative process and criteria for the assessment of creativity. He goes on to deal with creativity as a personality-affective-emotional phenomenon and as a cognitive procedure. Procedures are then reviewed for developing the preparatory stage of creativity, the hypothesis formation stage, hypothesis testing, and communicating results.

In Volume 2, Stein focuses on such group procedures as brainstorming, creative problem solving, synectics, and various other programs. A research study is also presented in considerable detail in which cognitive and personality approaches to stimulating creativity were compared. The conclusion of the study is that both the cognitive and personality aspects are vital in developing creative thinking ability.

TEACHING THE GIFTED CHILD (2nd EDITION)

James J. Gallagher
1975
List price: $17.95
How to order: Allyn & Bacon
470 Atlantic Avenue
Boston, Massachusetts
02210

This is the leading text in gifted education. It is both a text and a basic reference since it covers the field comprehensively. This text covers the usual topics of characteristics and identification of the gifted, school programs, administration, and training personnel for work with the gifted. There are also four chapters covering mathematics, science, social studies and language arts for the gifted. Two chapters are devoted to creativity and problem solving. Finally, there are excellent chapters on gifted underachievers and the culturally different gifted child. The author also provides a set of case histories that are used to illustrate some of the major behavioral characteristics of gifted students. Each of the chapters ends with a statement of unresolved issues and a list of suggestions for further reading. Appendices offer lists of information resources, materials, and organizations for gifted education.

YELLOW PAGES OF LEARNING RESOURCES

Richard S. Wurman (ed.)
1972
List price: $2.95
How to order: The MIT Press
              Massachusetts Institute of Technology
              Cambridge, Massachusetts 02142

Yellow Pages of Learning Resources is a book full of questions which invite the child to discover the city as a learning resource. By planting the seed of inquiry (e.g., what can you learn from a carpenter? at a cemetery? from a dry cleaner? from a locksmith?), *Yellow Pages of Learning Resources* stimulates the curiosity of children and builds a desire to go and find out what one *can* learn from a carpenter, at a cemetery, or from a dry cleaner.

Children, high school students, parents, and teachers will all find this attractive book (it looks like a telephone directory with advertisements) full of ideas and questions that can be answered in the city. Besides the classroom and teachers, the most valuable resources for learning are people, places, and the processes of the cities, towns, or villages in which we live. This book helps teachers and children use those resources.

It is an attractive and stimulating resource book.